MILITARY AND VETERAN ISSUES

MAJOR DEPRESSIVE DISORDER IN VETERANS

ANTIDEPRESSANT USE AND SUICIDE PREVENTION

MILITARY AND VETERAN ISSUES

Additional books in this series can be found on Nova's website under the Series tab.

Additional e-books in this series can be found on Nova's website under the e-book tab.

MILITARY AND VETERAN ISSUES

MAJOR DEPRESSIVE DISORDER IN VETERANS

ANTIDEPRESSANT USE AND SUICIDE PREVENTION

CASEY P. BARTON
EDITOR

NOVINKA
New York

NOTICE TO THE READER

The Publisher has taken reasonable care in the preparation of this book, but makes no expressed or implied warranty of any kind and assumes no responsibility for any errors or omissions. No liability is assumed for incidental or consequential damages in connection with or arising out of information contained in this book. The Publisher shall not be liable for any special, consequential, or exemplary damages resulting, in whole or in part, from the readers' use of, or reliance upon, this material. Any parts of this book based on government reports are so indicated and copyright is claimed for those parts to the extent applicable to compilations of such works.

Independent verification should be sought for any data, advice or recommendations contained in this book. In addition, no responsibility is assumed by the publisher for any injury and/or damage to persons or property arising from any methods, products, instructions, ideas or otherwise contained in this publication.

This publication is designed to provide accurate and authoritative information with regard to the subject matter covered herein. It is sold with the clear understanding that the Publisher is not engaged in rendering legal or any other professional services. If legal or any other expert assistance is required, the services of a competent person should be sought. FROM A DECLARATION OF PARTICIPANTS JOINTLY ADOPTED BY A COMMITTEE OF THE AMERICAN BAR ASSOCIATION AND A COMMITTEE OF PUBLISHERS.

Additional color graphics may be available in the e-book version of this book.

Library of Congress Cataloging-in-Publication Data

ISBN: 978-1-63482-561-0

Published by Nova Science Publishers, Inc. † New York

CONTENTS

PREFACE

In 2013, the Department of Veterans Affairs (VA) estimated that about 1.5 million veterans required mental health care, including services for Major Depressive Disorder (MDD). MDD is a debilitating mental illness related to reduced quality of life and productivity, and increased risk for suicide. VA also plays a role in suicide prevention. This book begins with a brief overview of the public health framework for suicide prevention, which forms the basis for both the National Strategy for Suicide Prevention and the VHA's approach to suicide prevention. The book discusses suicide surveillance; suicide risk factors and protective factors; suicide prevention interventions; potential issues for Congress; VA's data on veterans with MDD, including those prescribed an antidepressant; the extent that veterans with MDD who are prescribed antidepressants receive recommended care and the extent to which VA monitors such care; and the quality of data VA requires VAMCs to collect on veteran suicides.

Chapter 1 – This report focuses on suicide prevention activities of the Veterans Health Administration (VHA) within the Department of Veterans Affairs (VA). The VHA's approach to suicide prevention is based on a public health framework, which has three major components: (1) surveillance, (2) risk and protective factors, and (3) interventions.

Surveillance, or systematic collection of data on completed (i.e., fatal) suicides, is essential to define the scope of the problem (i.e., the suicide rate among veterans), identify characteristics associated with higher or lower risk of suicide, and track changes in the suicide rate. No nationwide surveillance system exists for suicide among all veterans. Information about deaths (including suicides) is collected in death certificates by state, territorial, and local governments. Death certificate data are aggregated into the National Death Index, which can be combined with data about who is a veteran to identify veteran suicides. The VHA collects detailed information about suicides among veterans that are known to VHA facilities; however, the majority of veterans are not enrolled in VHA health care, so other sources of information (e.g., Department of Defense data) are necessary to identify veterans.

Information collected in surveillance is used to identify suicide risk factors (i.e., characteristics associated with higher rates of suicide) and protective factors (i.e., characteristics associated with lower rates of suicide). This is essential in order to design interventions that reduce risk factors and/or increase protective factors, thus lowering overall risk of suicide. Risk factors are also helpful in identifying at-risk groups or individuals so that interventions can be delivered to the people who need them most. Within the VHA, this research is supported by the Office of Research and Development; a Center of Excellence in suicide prevention; and a Mental Illness Research, Education, and Clinical Center on suicide prevention.

The intervention cycle includes three stages: (1) design and test interventions, (2) implement interventions, and (3) evaluate interventions. The research components mentioned above have roles in small-scale pilot testing and large-scale evaluations of interventions. VHA suicide prevention interventions include easy access to care, screening and treatment, suicide prevention coordinators, suicide hotline, education and outreach, and limited access to lethal means.

The VHA has received both praise and criticism for its suicide prevention efforts and mental health services more generally. A 2010 progress report on the National Strategy for Suicide Prevention describes the VHA as "one of the most vibrant forces in the U.S. suicide prevention movement, implementing multiple levels of innovation and state of the art interventions, backed up by a robust evaluation and research capacity." In contrast, some have testified before Congress that VHA's suicide prevention efforts have inadequacies, such as barriers to accessing care and lack of evidence-based treatments for those who do access care. A 2011 evaluation of VHA mental health services captures both sides of the argument, finding that VHA mental health care is generally at least as good as that of other health care systems, but that it "often does not meet implicit VA expectations."

Potential issues for Congress and related recommendations by outside organizations fall into three categories: improving the timeliness and accuracy of surveillance data, building the evidence base, and increasing access to evidence-based mental health care. Public laws addressing suicide prevention among veterans are described in the *Appendix*.

Chapter 2 – This is a Statement of Dr. Harold Kudler, Chief Mental Health Consultant, Veterans Health Administration. Hearing on "Mental Health and Suicide Among Veterans" before the Senate Committee on Veterans Affairs, dated November 19, 2014.

Chapter 3 – In 2013, VA estimated that about 1.5 million veterans required mental health care, including services for MDD. MDD is a debilitating mental illness related to reduced quality of life and productivity, and increased risk for suicide. VA also plays a role in suicide prevention. GAO was asked to review how VA tracks veterans prescribed antidepressants and what suicide data VA uses in its prevention efforts.

This report examines (1) VA's data on veterans with MDD, including those prescribed an antidepressant; (2) the extent that veterans with MDD who are prescribed antidepressants receive recommended care and the extent to which VA monitors such care; and (3) the quality of data VA requires VAMCs to collect on veteran suicides. GAO analyzed VA data, interviewed VA officials, and conducted site visits to six VAMCs selected based on geography and population served. From each of these six VAMCs, GAO also reviewed five randomly selected medical records for veterans diagnosed with MDD and prescribed an antidepressant in 2012, as well as all completed BHAP templates. The results cannot be generalized across VA but provide insights.

In: Major Depressive Disorder in Veterans
Editor: Casey P. Barton
ISBN: 978-1-63482-561-0

Chapter 1

HEALTH CARE FOR VETERANS: SUICIDE PREVENTION*

Erin Bagalman

SUMMARY

This report focuses on suicide prevention activities of the Veterans Health Administration (VHA) within the Department of Veterans Affairs (VA). The VHA's approach to suicide prevention is based on a public health framework, which has three major components: (1) surveillance, (2) risk and protective factors, and (3) interventions.

Surveillance, or systematic collection of data on completed (i.e., fatal) suicides, is essential to define the scope of the problem (i.e., the suicide rate among veterans), identify characteristics associated with higher or lower risk of suicide, and track changes in the suicide rate. No nationwide surveillance system exists for suicide among all veterans. Information about deaths (including suicides) is collected in death certificates by state, territorial, and local governments. Death certificate data are aggregated into the National Death Index, which can be combined with data about who is a veteran to identify veteran suicides. The VHA collects detailed information about suicides among veterans that are known to VHA facilities; however, the majority of veterans are

* This is an edited, reformatted and augmented version of a Congressional Research Service publication R42340, prepared for Members and Committees of Congress dated January 30, 2015.

not enrolled in VHA health care, so other sources of information (e.g., Department of Defense data) are necessary to identify veterans.

Information collected in surveillance is used to identify suicide risk factors (i.e., characteristics associated with higher rates of suicide) and protective factors (i.e., characteristics associated with lower rates of suicide). This is essential in order to design interventions that reduce risk factors and/or increase protective factors, thus lowering overall risk of suicide. Risk factors are also helpful in identifying at-risk groups or individuals so that interventions can be delivered to the people who need them most. Within the VHA, this research is supported by the Office of Research and Development; a Center of Excellence in suicide prevention; and a Mental Illness Research, Education, and Clinical Center on suicide prevention.

The intervention cycle includes three stages: (1) design and test interventions, (2) implement interventions, and (3) evaluate interventions. The research components mentioned above have roles in small-scale pilot testing and large-scale evaluations of interventions. VHA suicide prevention interventions include easy access to care, screening and treatment, suicide prevention coordinators, suicide hotline, education and outreach, and limited access to lethal means.

The VHA has received both praise and criticism for its suicide prevention efforts and mental health services more generally. A 2010 progress report on the National Strategy for Suicide Prevention describes the VHA as "one of the most vibrant forces in the U.S. suicide prevention movement, implementing multiple levels of innovation and state of the art interventions, backed up by a robust evaluation and research capacity." In contrast, some have testified before Congress that VHA's suicide prevention efforts have inadequacies, such as barriers to accessing care and lack of evidence-based treatments for those who do access care. A 2011 evaluation of VHA mental health services captures both sides of the argument, finding that VHA mental health care is generally at least as good as that of other health care systems, but that it "often does not meet implicit VA expectations."

Potential issues for Congress and related recommendations by outside organizations fall into three categories: improving the timeliness and accuracy of surveillance data, building the evidence base, and increasing access to evidence-based mental health care. Public laws addressing suicide prevention among veterans are described in the *Appendix*.

Congress has attempted to address the problem of suicide among veterans through legislation[1] and oversight hearings,[2] both on prevention of veteran suicide specifically and on veteran mental health more broadly. A task as challenging as preventing suicide requires collaboration among federal agencies, state and local governments, other organizations, communities, and individuals. This report, however, focuses on activities of the Veterans Health Administration (VHA) within the Department of Veterans Affairs (VA). The VHA's approach to suicide prevention is based in part on the National Strategy for Suicide Prevention,[3] which involves multiple federal departments, including the VA, Defense (DOD), and Education (ED), as well as several agencies within Health and Human Services (HHS).[4] While this CRS report focuses on suicide prevention efforts of the VHA, activities of other entities are discussed as they relate to VHA activities.

This CRS report begins with a brief overview of the public health framework for suicide prevention, which forms the basis for both the National Strategy for Suicide Prevention and the VHA's approach to suicide prevention. The three subsequent parts of the report correspond to the three major components of the public health framework: (1) suicide surveillance, (2) suicide risk factors and protective factors, and (3) suicide prevention interventions. The final section addresses potential issues for Congress, and the *Appendix* summarizes provisions of public laws addressing suicide prevention among veterans.

A Public Health Framework for Suicide Prevention

Prevention of suicide can be approached in two ways, which are not mutually exclusive. The public health approach intervenes with populations (e.g., distributing educational materials about mental illness and mental health services), whereas the clinical approach intervenes with individuals (e.g., prescribing antidepressant medication to a person diagnosed with depression). The individual focus of the clinical approach limits its reach to those who access the health care system;[5] clinical interventions are necessary but not sufficient. The population-based public health approach is considered essential to address the broader problem of suicide among all veterans, including those who may not currently be in contact with the health care system.

Both the National Strategy for Suicide Prevention and the VHA's approach to suicide prevention are based on a public health framework. As illustrated in *Figure 1*, the framework has three major components: (1) surveillance, (2) risk and protective factors, and (3) prevention interventions.

Suicide surveillance involves collecting data on completed (i.e., fatal) suicides in order to define the scope of the problem. Data collected in surveillance can be used to identify risk factors (i.e., characteristics associated with higher suicide risk) and protective factors (i.e., characteristics associated with lower suicide risk). Suicide prevention interventions aim to reduce risk factors and/or enhance protective factors that have been identified; interventions may target high-risk groups or individuals, identified based on known risk factors.

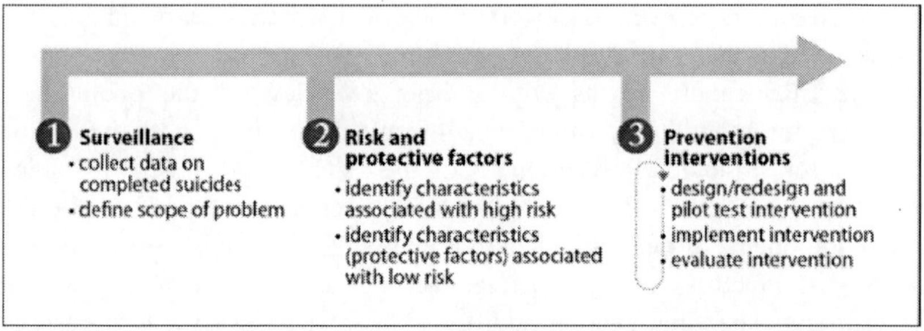

Source: CRS analysis of major components of U.S. Department of Health and Human Services (HHS) Office of the Surgeon General and National Action Alliance for Suicide Prevention, 2012 National Strategy for Suicide Prevention: Goals and Objectives for Action, Washington DC: HHS, September 2012.

Figure 1.A Public Health Framework for Suicide Prevention.

VHA SUICIDE SURVEILLANCE

No nationwide surveillance system exists for suicide among all veterans. Surveillance, or systematic collection of data on completed (i.e., fatal) suicides, is essential for three purposes.

First, surveillance defines the scope of the problem, that is, the suicide rate among veterans.

Second, information from surveillance is used to identify characteristics associated with higher or lower risk of suicide.

Third, information from surveillance is used to track changes in the suicide rate and evaluate suicide prevention interventions. In order to evaluate interventions, suicide surveillance must measure the same thing, in the same way, repeatedly over time. In the case of veteran suicide, surveillance requires identifying both who is a veteran and who has died by suicide.

The VHA collects detailed information about suicides (and suicide attempts) among veterans *that are known to VHA facilities*. The VHA's Behavioral Health Autopsy Program (BHAP)—which began in December 2012 and has not yet been fully implemented—will eventually collect information on suicides that are known to the VHA in four phases. The VHA has already implemented the first two phases: standardized chart reviews and interviews with family members.

The third and fourth phases include interviewing the last clinician to see the veteran and locating public records that might indicate stressors (e.g., bankruptcy or divorce). A Government Accountability Office (GAO) evaluation found that some BHAP reports were not submitted, that some included inaccurate information, and that more than half of those reviewed were incomplete. The GAO also found that VHA facilities had interpreted BHAP instructions differently and that no VHA or VA officials were reviewing BHAP reports for accuracy or completeness.[6]

Resolving the problems the GAO identified with BHAP would result in better information about suicides among veterans that are known to VHA facilities; however, information collected solely by the VHA would still exclude suicides among other veterans (i.e., those who are not known to the VHA). Of more than 21 million veterans estimated to live in the United States, fewer than 10 million are enrolled to receive health care from the VHA.[7] The VA also has records of veterans who receive other benefits (e.g., home loans), regardless of whether they are enrolled in VHA health care, but does not have records of all veterans. The VA is working with the DOD to identify suicides among all veterans, including those who do not interact with the VA.

Information about deaths—including whether a death resulted from intentional self-harm (i.e., suicide)—is collected in death certificates by state, territorial, and local governments.[8] The resulting data may not be comparable across jurisdictions.[9]

The Centers for Disease Control and Prevention (CDC) aggregates death certificate data into the National Death Index (NDI), which can then be combined with data about who is a veteran.[10] The lag between a suicide event and identification of the decedent as a veteran may be years; this delays the availability of crucial information. Timely reporting of death certificates was identified as a core issue in a 2010 progress report on an earlier version (2001) of the National Strategy for Suicide Prevention.[11]

VHA RESEARCH INTO RISK AND PROTECTIVE FACTORS

Identifying characteristics associated with higher rates of suicide (i.e., risk factors) and lower rates of suicide (i.e., protective factors) is essential in order to design effective interventions.

Suicide prevention interventions aim to reduce risk factors and/or increase protective factors, thus lowering overall risk of suicide. Knowing what the risk factors are also helps in identifying at-risk groups or individuals so that interventions can be delivered to the people who need them most. Thus the second step in the public health framework for suicide prevention is identification of suicide risk and protective factors. *Table 1* provides examples of risk and protective factors among the general population.

Table 1. Selected Risk and Protective Factors in the General Population

Risk Factors	Protective Factors
Some major physical illnesses, mental disorders, and substance use disorders	Effective clinical care for physical illnesses, mental disorders, and substance use disorders
Barriers to accessing health care	Easy access to a variety of clinical interventions
Stigma associated with help-seeking behavior	Support for help-seeking behavior
Easy access to lethal means (e.g., firearms or poison)	Restricted access to lethal means (e.g., firearms or poison)
Lack of social support and sense of isolation	Strong connections to family and community support
Cultural/religious beliefs that accept suicide	Cultural/religious beliefs that discourage suicide

Source: Examples of risk and protective factors selected from U.S. Department of Health and Human Services (HHS), Centers for Disease Control and Prevention (CDC), Injury Center: Violence Prevention, Suicide: Risk and Protective Factors, http://www.cdc.gov/violenceprevention/suicide/riskprotectivefactors.html.

Veteran-specific research on suicide risk and protective factors is necessary because the veteran population differs from the non-veteran population on a variety of characteristics (e.g., gender distribution), some of which may also be associated with suicide risk. For example, research has explored whether combat exposure is associated with risk of suicide (with mixed results).12 The subpopulation of veterans who are enrolled with the VHA may differ from non-enrolled veterans, as well.

The VHA conducts veteran-specific research that builds on research among the general population. Within HHS, both the CDC13 and the National Institute of Mental Health (NIMH)14 disseminate research on suicide risk and protective factors within the general population. Also, the Substance Abuse and Mental Health Services Administration (SAMHSA) collects data on suicide attempts and related behavior.15 It should be noted that risk factors for attempted suicide may differ from risk factors for completed suicide; for example, women have a higher rate of attempted suicide, but men have a higher rate of completed suicide.16 Despite a large number of risk and protective factors identified by researchers, it is not yet possible to predict who will attempt or complete suicide.17 The inability to identify individuals most in need of interventions is one of the reasons a public health approach—with a focus on population-level interventions—is necessary for effective suicide prevention.

Within the VHA, mental health research—including research on suicide risk and protective factors—is supported by three research components: the Office of Research and Development (ORD), a Center of Excellence (COE) in suicide prevention, and a Mental Illness Research, Education, and Clinical Center (MIRECC) on suicide prevention. Administratively, both the COE and the MIRECC (as well as other centers) fall under the Mental Health Strategic Healthcare Group, which is a separate organizational unit from ORD. Examples of research conducted on risk and protective factors by each of these three components—ORD, COE, and MIRECC—are provided below.

VHA Office of Research and Development (ORD)

In general, the ORD funds intramural research by individual VHA investigators or researchers (including mental health care research).[18] The ORD's Health Services Research and Development Service supports research into suicide risk factors and protective factors.[19] For example, the VHA conducted a study of suicide risk among veterans with depression (a known risk factor in the general population, as well as among veterans).[20] Another study examined characteristics associated with suicide risk among patients seen in VHA primary care, to help identify factors that primary care providers may be able to use to detect suicide risk.[21] These studies, and others like them, can help the VHA identify veterans at high risk of suicide, so that interventions can be targeted to them.

Center of Excellence (COE)

The COE at Canandaigua, NY, conducts research on suicide risk factors and protective factors, in addition to other suicide prevention activities. Established in August 2007 at the direction of Congress,[22] the COE has the mission of developing and studying evidence-based public health approaches to prevention of veteran suicide, with the goal of reducing morbidity and mortality associated with suicide in the veteran population. In pursuit of its mission, the Epidemiology and Interventions Research Core within the COE collects and analyzes data on suicide risk factors and protective factors (as well as other topics) among both veterans who use VHA services and those who do not.[23]

Mental Illness Research, Education, and Clinical Center (MIRECC)

The MIRECCs, also established at the direction of Congress,[24] conduct research on a range of mental health-related topics, including suicide risk factors and protective factors. Specifically, the MIRECC of the VA Rocky Mountain Network pursues the goal of reducing suicidality in the veteran population, by conducting research on potential contributions of cognitive and neurobiological factors, among other activities.[25] For example, one study assesses the relationship (if any) between suicidal ideation and thinking under stress.[26] Another study investigates cognitive functioning, distress, and suicide risk in Veterans with HIV/AIDS.[27] Other MIRECCs may also conduct research related to suicide, in the course of pursuing their other goals.

SELECTED VHA SUICIDE PREVENTION INTERVENTIONS

Suicide prevention interventions aim to reduce risk factors and/or enhance protective factors, thereby lowering the risk of suicide. They may address entire populations (e.g., all veterans), at-risk subgroups (e.g., veterans diagnosed with a mental disorder), or high-risk individuals (e.g., veterans with recent suicide attempts).

Interventions are refined in a three-stage cycle. The first stage is to develop and pilot test interventions on a small scale to ensure that they are safe, ethical, feasible, efficacious (i.e., they work under ideal conditions), and effective (i.e., they work under real-world conditions). If interventions are successful in the first stage, the second stage is to implement them on a larger scale. The third stage is to evaluate interventions that have been implemented on a larger scale, to verify their effectiveness and determine for whom they are most effective. The three stages can then be repeated to refine interventions, either to improve their effectiveness or to adjust them for use with a different population (e.g., applying an intervention developed for male veterans to a population of female veterans).

Within the VHA, the same three research components involved in risk and protective factors research are involved in the intervention cycle: ORD,[28] COE,[29] and MIRECC.[30] Because small-scale testing and large-scale evaluation are both integral to suicide prevention interventions, it is worth noting that rigorous research on effectiveness is difficult and lacking for most interventions, both within and outside the VHA.[31]

Easy Access to Care

Easy access to care is a protective factor against suicide, and the VHA is making efforts to increase access to care by addressing known barriers to care, including lack of understanding or awareness of mental health care, stigma associated with mental illness, and concerns about VHA care, and challenges in scheduling appointments.[32] The VHA provides information to help increase awareness of mental health care services, reduce the stigma associated with seeking care, and correct misconceptions about VHA care.[33] Some mental health and substance use evaluation and treatment services have been integrated into other treatment settings, which both increases the convenience and reduces the stigma associated with seeking care.[34]

VHA policy requires that emergency mental health care be available 24 hours per day through emergency rooms at VA facilities or local, non-VA hospitals;[35] that new patients referred for mental health services receive an initial assessment within 24 hours and a full evaluation appointment within 14 days; and that follow-up appointments for established patients be scheduled within 30 days.[36] The extent to which these policies are implemented in practice has been questioned in congressional testimony,[37] news media,[38] and survey responses from both providers and patients.[39]

Screening and Treatment

Some types of screening, pharmacotherapy, and psychotherapy are supported by evidence that they reduce the likelihood of suicide.[40] VHA policy requires screening for a variety of risk factors, including but not limited to posttraumatic stress disorder (PTSD), depression, and alcohol abuse. Those who screen positive are evaluated further and offered treatment if found to have a mental health problem. Positive screens for PTSD or depression, in particular, are followed by a suicide risk assessment.[41]

An evaluation of VHA mental health care by the Altarum Institute and RAND Health finds that treatment in the VHA is generally better than in other systems on a variety of measures, but still has room for improvement.[42] In particular, the evaluation finds that evidence-based treatments (both pharmacotherapy and psychotherapy), while widely available, are not usually provided.[43] Researchers based this finding on a review of medical records, which showed that prescriptions for medication were often not filled for as long as recommended and that psychotherapy, as documented, was often not delivered according to evidence-based guidelines. Additionally, the evaluation found that assessment is lacking, both at the beginning of treatment and during treatment (to track progress).[44] Even if a particular treatment is supported by evidence, it will not necessarily be effective for every patient. The only way to know whether a patient is improving, holding steady, or growing worse is to assess his or her symptoms at intervals.

Suicide Prevention Coordinators

Per department policy, every VA Medical Center has at least one suicide prevention coordinator, whose responsibilities include (among other things) tracking patients who have been identified as at high risk for suicide. The VHA's computerized patient record system enables clinicians to flag high-risk patients, and policy requires that safety plans be developed for them.[45] A safety plan is a written document developed jointly by a patient and a clinician that identifies strategies for coping in a crisis (e.g., recognizing warning signs and contacting family members, friends, or mental health providers). Outside the VHA, the use of suicide prevention coordinators has not been widely adopted, although some components of the program (e.g., safety plans) are widely used. The suicide prevention coordinator program has been identified as a practice worth emulating by a DOD task force on suicide prevention.[46]

Suicide Hotline

Suicide hotlines are telephone numbers individuals can call for help in crisis situations (e.g., at the moment they are considering suicide). Hotlines are generally toll-free and available around the clock. The Veterans Crisis Line is a joint effort of the VHA and SAMHSA.[47] The main line (1 800-273-8255) is the National Suicide Prevention Lifeline, operated by SAMHSA.[48] Veterans (or others calling with concerns about veterans) may select option 1 to be directed to the VHA's Veterans Crisis Line, answered by staff at the COE in Canandaigua, NY. Callers may remain anonymous or disclose their identities in order to allow the COE staff to access their VA medical records during the call. The Veterans Crisis Line is supplemented by an online chat service (http://www.VeteransCrisisLine.net/chat) and support via text messaging (text 838255). The Veterans Crisis Line has answered more than 1.25 million calls since it began in 2007, has engaged in more than 175,000 chats since it added the chat service in 2009, and has responded to more than 24,000 texts since it added the text-messaging service in 2011.[49]

The evidence base for suicide hotlines is not sufficient to determine their effectiveness in reducing suicide rates, due to the difficulties inherent in conducting such evaluations.[50] The confidentiality of suicide hotlines renders follow-up with each individual caller impossible. Moreover, national hotlines, such as those operated by SAMHSA and the VHA, serve a large geographic area. A range of other interventions may be in place in localities within the hotline's reach, such that any change in the suicide rate may not be attributable to the hotline.

Education and Outreach

The VHA offers suicide prevention education and outreach to staff, patients, and surrounding communities. All VHA health care providers are required to complete web-based training on suicide risk and intervention and to pass a post-test.[51] VHA Suicide Prevention Coordinators are required to conduct outreach activities in their local communities.[52] The VHA has co-sponsored (with the Department of Defense) conferences on suicide prevention to educate clinicians and has sponsored Suicide Prevention Days to raise awareness. Efforts to promote the Veterans Crisis Line (e.g., public service announcements and distribution of brochures, wallet cards, key chains, etc.) also help raise awareness.

Limited Access to Lethal Means

The three most common means of completing suicide among the general population are firearms (50%), suffocation (24%), and poisoning (18%).[53] Evidence supports restricting access to lethal means (e.g., firearms, gas, drugs) as a way to reduce suicide rates.[54] The VHA has a gun safety program (as both a child safety initiative and a suicide prevention initiative), which includes distribution of free gun locks and dissemination of gun safety information.[55] The VHA also conducts research on blister packaging medications as a potential way to reduce the incidence of medication overdoses.[56]

Potential Issues for Congress

The VHA has received both praise and criticism for its suicide prevention efforts and mental health services more generally. A 2010 progress report on an earlier version (2001) of the National Strategy for Suicide Prevention praises VHA's suicide prevention practices and recommends disseminating them to the rest of the health care system, describing the VHA as "one of the most vibrant forces in the U.S. suicide prevention movement, implementing multiple levels of innovation and state of the art interventions, backed up by a robust evaluation and research capacity."[57] In contrast, some congressional testimony has criticized VHA's suicide prevention efforts for inadequacies, such as barriers to accessing care and lack of evidence-based treatments for those who do access care.[58] A 2011 evaluation of VHA mental health services (not limited to suicide prevention efforts) by the Altarum Institute and RAND Health captures both sides of the argument, finding that VHA mental health care is generally at least as good as that of other health care systems, but that it "often does not meet implicit VA expectations."[59]

Potential issues for Congress and related recommendations by outside organizations fall into three categories: improving the timeliness and accuracy of surveillance data, building the evidence base, and increasing access to evidence-based mental health care.

Improving the Timeliness and Accuracy of Surveillance Data

Challenges in suicide surveillance include timeliness of data, consistent classification of deaths as suicides, and accuracy of information. Addressing these challenges requires the involvement of entities other than VHA.

Recommendations related to the timeliness of suicide surveillance data include ensuring that the CDC's ability to compile national death data expeditiously is not limited by a lack of resources; coordinating the annual analysis of veteran suicide data among VA, DOD, and HHS; and establishing "reasonable time requirements for states to provide death data to the CDC."[60] It should be noted that states, territories, and cities *voluntarily* share vital statistics with the CDC, so offering incentives for timely data might be more feasible than imposing requirements.

It is widely believed that inconsistent reporting of suicides across jurisdictions, as well as underreporting of suicides in general, limits the effectiveness of surveillance efforts.[61] Classification of a death as a suicide requires a determination that the death is both self-inflicted and intentional. Determining the decedent's intent is difficult, and coroners or medical examiners may feel pressure not to classify a death as suicide, due to the stigma associated with suicide. Suicides may be underreported when the manner of death is misclassified as "undetermined" or "accidental" (e.g., poisonings or single-vehicle crashes). Additionally, each jurisdiction (state, territory, or city) has its own requirements for investigating deaths, leading to variability across jurisdictions.

The GAO recommends that the VA implement processes to improve the completeness, accuracy, and consistency of data reported through the VHA's Behavioral Health Autopsy Program (BHAP) system.[62] Beyond that, the VA must rely on outside data sources (e.g., the DOD) to identify decedents as veterans if they are enrolled with the agency.[63]

Building the Evidence Base

Developing an adequate evidence base is necessary both to identify risk and protective factors and to develop and disseminate effective interventions. Recommendations include increased information sharing, collaboration, and dialogue across areas of public health, among government agencies, and between congressional committees.

Suicide prevention tends to operate in its own silo, even though suicide has some of the same risk and protective factors as other public health problems. Increased collaboration and dialogue between suicide prevention and other areas of public health "will help prevent the field from endlessly recreating wheels and spreading the limited funds too broadly to make a sustainable difference."[64]

If agencies (federal, state, or local) engage in ongoing collaboration and dialogue, sharing evaluations of existing interventions and research into new interventions, they may prevent unnecessary duplication of effort and help build the evidence base more quickly.[65] (Note that replication of studies is an integral part of the research process, so a distinction may be made between appropriate and unnecessary duplication of effort.) Specific recommendations include sharing research findings (e.g., risk and protective factors) between the VA, DOD, and HHS[66] and fast-tracking all phases of the intervention cycle (designing and pilot testing interventions, implementing interventions, and evaluating interventions), as well as the dissemination of the knowledge gained in each phase.[67]

Some have also recommended that the House and Senate Committees on Veterans' Affairs initiate discussions with the House and Senate Armed Services Committees to develop provisions addressing veteran suicide in the National Defense Authorization Act.[68]

Increasing Access to High-Quality Mental Health Care

Providing timely access to high-quality mental health care has been a challenge for the VHA. The Veterans Access, Choice, and Accountability Act of 2014 (P.L. 113-146 , as amended) aims to increase access and decrease wait times for veterans seeking VHA care (not limited to mental health care).[69] Among other things, the act establishes the Veterans Choice Program, which requires the VHA to authorize reimbursement for non-VHA care under specified conditions. One such condition occurs when a qualified veteran is unable to schedule an appointment within the VHA's wait-time goals. In accordance with Act, the VHA has established a wait-time goal "to furnish care within 30 days of either the date that an appointment is deemed clinically appropriate by a VA health care provider, or if no such clinical determination has been made, the date a veteran prefers to be seen."[70]

When veterans gain access to care—within or outside the VHA—they may not always receive high-quality care.[71] While the VHA has made progress in disseminating knowledge about evidence-based treatment (e.g., through clinical practice guidelines developed jointly with DOD), that does not guarantee implementation or such treatments.[72] A 2014 report by the RAND Corporation indicates that only 13% of mental health providers in the study met criteria for readiness to provide veteran-friendly, high-quality care.[73] Providers working within the VHA or a military setting were more likely than others to meet the criteria, which may raise questions for some about increasing the use of non-VHA care. The report includes recommendations to conduct better assessments of civilian provider capacity, assess the impact of trainings in cultural competency on provider capacity, expand access to effective trainings in selected evidence-based approaches, and facilitate providers' use of evidence-based approaches.

APPENDIX. PUBLIC LAWS ADDRESSING VA SUICIDE PREVENTION EFFORTS

Since Operations Enduring Freedom and Iraqi Freedom began, four public laws have addressed VHA suicide prevention efforts: the Joshua Omvig Veterans Suicide Prevention Act (P.L. 110- 110); the National Defense Authorization Act for Fiscal Year 2008 (P.L. 110-181); the Veterans' Benefits Improvement Act of 2008 (P.L. 110-389); and the Caregivers and Veterans Omnibus Health Services Act of 2010 (P.L. 111-163). Relevant provisions of each are summarized below.

Joshua Omvig Veterans Suicide Prevention Act

The Joshua Omvig Veterans Suicide Prevention Act (P.L. 110-110), enacted in 2007, required the VA Secretary to develop and implement a comprehensive suicide prevention program, and to report to Congress on the program. The Congressional Budget Office estimated that implementing the Joshua Omvig Veterans Suicide Prevention Act would have "little, if any, cost," because the VA already had implemented or was planning to implement each of the specific requirements.[74] The textbox below lists the required elements and additional authorized elements of the comprehensive suicide prevention program.

Joshua Omvig Veterans Suicide Prevention Act (P.L. 110-110) Required elements of the comprehensive suicide prevention program include the following:

- mandatory suicide prevention training for appropriate VA staff and contractors;
- designation of a suicide prevention counselor at each VA medical center;
- outreach and education for veterans and their families to promote mental health;
- mental health assessments of veterans and referrals to appropriate treatment;
- availability of 24-hour mental health care for veterans;
- research on best practices for suicide prevention; and
- research on mental health among veterans with military sexual trauma.

Additional authorized (but not required) elements include the following:

- a 24-hour toll-free hotline staffed by trained mental health personnel;
- peer support counseling; and
- other actions to reduce the incidence of suicide among veterans.

National Defense Authorization Act for Fiscal Year 2008

Section 1611 of the National Defense Authorization Act for Fiscal Year 2008 (P.L. 110-181) directed the VA and DOD Secretaries to jointly develop a comprehensive care and transition policy for servicemembers recovering from serious injuries or illnesses related to their military service. The law specified that the policy must address (among other things) the training and skills of health care professionals, recovery coordinators, and case managers, to ensure that they are able to detect and report early warning signs of suicidal thoughts or behaviors, along with other behavioral health concerns. The law further specified that the policy must include tracking the notifications made by recovery care coordinators, medical care case managers, and nonmedical care managers to health care professionals regarding suicidal thoughts or behaviors, along with other behavioral health concerns. A 2009 Government Accountability Office report indicates that DOD and VA have developed the relevant policies.[75]

Veterans' Benefits Improvement Act of 2008

Section 809 of the Veterans' Benefits Improvement Act of 2008 (P.L. 110-389) grants the VA Secretary authority to advertise in the media for various purposes, including suicide prevention.

Caregivers and Veterans Omnibus Health Services Act of 2010

Section 403 of the Caregivers and Veterans Omnibus Health Services Act of 2010 (P.L. 111-163) requires the VA Secretary to conduct a study to determine the number of veterans who died by suicide between January 1, 1999, and May 5, 2010 (i.e., the date of enactment). The in-progress study, dubbed the State Mortality Data Project, is described in a VA report published in February 2013.[76]

End Notes

[1] See the *Appendix* for public laws addressing suicide among veterans.

[2] See, for example, U.S. Congress, Senate Committee on Veterans' Affairs, *VA Mental Health Care: Ensuring Timely Access to High-Quality Care*, 113th Cong., 1st sess., March 20, 2013; U.S. Congress, House Committee on Veterans' Affairs, Subcommittee on Health, *Service Should Not Lead to Suicide: Access to VA's Mental Health Care*, 113th Cong., 2nd sess., July 10, 2014; and U.S. Congress, Senate Committee on Veterans' Affairs, *Mental Health and Suicide Among Veterans*, 113th Cong., 2nd sess., November 19, 2014.

[3] U.S. Department of Health and Human Services (HHS) Office of the Surgeon General and National Action Alliance for Suicide Prevention, *2012 National Strategy for Suicide Prevention: Goals and Objectives for Action*, Washington DC: HHS, September 2012,

http://www.surgeongeneral.gov/library/reports/national-strategy-suicide-prevention; hereinafter referred to as *National Strategy for Suicide Prevention*.

[4] Federal Working Group on Suicide Prevention, *National Strategy for Suicide Prevention: Compendium of Federal Activities*, 2009. HHS agencies involved in suicide prevention include the Centers for Disease Control and Prevention (CDC), Indian Health Service (IHS), National Institute of Mental Health (NIMH), Substance Abuse and Mental Health Services Administration (SAMHSA), Health Resources and Services Administration (HRSA), Agency for Healthcare Research and Quality (AHRQ), and Administration on Aging (AoA).

[5] This report focuses on the public health approach. A full discussion of the clinical approach to suicide prevention is beyond the scope of this report. The pharmacotherapy and psychotherapy mentioned in the "Screening and Treatment" section are examples of the clinical approach.

[6] In addition to the BHAP, VA Medical Centers report data on *known* attempted and completed suicides (among other things) to the VA Central Office through the Suicide Prevention Application Network (SPAN). U.S. Government Accountability Office, *VA Health Care: Improvements Needed in Monitoring Antidepressant Use for Major Depressive Disorder and in Increasing Accuracy of Suicide Data*, GAO-15-55, December 12, 2014, http://www.gao.gov/products/ GAO-15-55.

[7] The estimated number of veterans living in the United States is from VetPop2011, at http://www.va.gov/vetdata/ Veteran_Population.asp. The estimated number of veterans enrolled in VHA health care is from the VA budget submission for FY2015, available at http://www.va.gov/budget/products.asp.

[8] Both the legal authority for maintaining registries of deaths and the responsibility for issuing death certificates reside with individual states, territories, and two cities (Washington, DC, and New York, NY).

[9] Researchers at the RAND Corporation summarized variation in suicide statistics across jurisdictions in four domains: (1) how suicides are defined or how ambiguous deaths are classified, (2) qualifications of professionals certifying a death as a suicide, (3) the extent to which possible suicide deaths are investigated, and (4) the quality of data management. Rajeev Ramchand et al., *The War Within: Preventing Suicide in the U.S. Military*, The RAND Corporation, 2011, p. 13, http://www.rand.org; hereinafter referred to as *The War Within*.

[10] CDC's National Center for Health Statistics (NCHS) works cooperatively with state, territorial, and local jurisdictions to collect information from death certificates in the National Vital Statistics System (NVSS). NCHS extracts information from NVSS to create the National Death Index (NDI), a data set that can be combined with other data sets for research purposes. For more information, see CDC, National Center for Health Statistics, *National Death*11 Suicide Prevention Resource Center and Suicide Prevention Action Network (SPAN), *Charting the Future of Suicide Prevention: A 2010 Progress Review of the National Strategy and Recommendations for the Decade Ahead*, 2010, p. 30; hereinafter referred to as *Charting the Future*.

[12] VA, VHA, National Center for PTSD, *The Relationship Between PTSD and Suicide*, last updated January 3, 2014, http://www.ptsd.va.gov/professional/co-occurring/ptsd-suicide.asp.

[13] Centers for Disease Control and Prevention, *Suicide: Risk and Protective Factors*, Atlanta, GA, http://www.cdc.gov/ ViolencePrevention/suicide/riskprotectivefactors.html.

[14] HHS, National Institutes of Health (NIH), National Institute of Mental Health, *Publications about Suicide Prevention*, http://www.nimh.nih.gov/health/publications/suicide-prevention-listing.shtml; and National Institute of Mental Health, *Science News about Suicide Prevention*, http://www.nimh.nih.gov/science-news/science-news-aboutsuicide-prevention.shtml.

[15] SAMHSA asks about these topics in the National Survey on Drug Use and Health (NSDUH). See HHS, CDC, *Morbidity and Mortality Weekly Report: Suicidal Thoughts and Behaviors Among Adults ≥ 18 Years—United States, 2008 – 2009*, October 21, 2011, http://www.cdc.gov/ mmwr/pdf/ss/ss6013.pdf.

[16] *National Strategy for Suicide Prevention, p. 18.*

[17] For example, although the single strongest predictor of a completed suicide is a prior suicide attempt, most people who attempt suicide do not subsequently complete suicide, and most people who complete suicides have no history of prior attempts. See *The War Within*, p. 29; and Joel Paris, "Predicting and Preventing Suicide: Do We Know Enough to Do Either?" *Harvard Review of Psychiatry*, vol. 14, no. 5 (2006), pp. 233-240.

[18] The ORD supports research through four research divisions: Biomedical Laboratory Research and Development (BLR&D), Clinical Science Research and Development (CSR&D), Rehabilitation Research and Development (RR&D), and Health Services Research and Development (HSR&D).

[19] A search for "suicide" at http://www.hsrd.research.va.gov/research/ yields dozens of suicide-related studies conducted within ORD's Health Services Research and Development (HSR&D) Service; some of the resulting studies investigate risk factors and/or protective factors.

[20] VA, VHA, Health Services Research and Development, *Risk of Death Among Veterans with Depression*, Study IIR 10-176, http://www.hsrd.research.va.gov/research/abstracts.cfm? Project_ID=2141701218.

[21] VA, VHA, Health Services Research and Development, *Veteran Interactions with VA Primary Care Prior to Suicide*, Study IIR 10-331, http://www.hsrd.research.va. gov/research/abstracts.cfm? Project_ID=2141701170.

[22] U.S. Congress, Committee of Conference, *Making Appropriations for Military Quality of Life Functions of the Department of Defense, Military Construction, the Department of Veterans Affairs, and Related Agencies for the Fiscal Year Ending September 30, 2006, and for Other Purposes*, report to accompany H.R. 2528, 109th Cong., 1st sess., November 18, 2005, H.Rept. 109-305 (Washington: GPO, 2006), p. 39. The committee report directed the VHA "to place more emphasis on psychiatric care of our veterans by designating three centers of excellence to focus on mental health/PTSD needs. These three centers will be established at Waco Medical Center, Texas; San Diego Medical Center, California; and the Canandaigua Medical Center, New York."

[23] VA, VHA, *VISN 2 Center of Excellence at Canandaigua*, http://www.mirecc.va.gov/docs/2010 InfoSheets/ VISN_2_CoE_Canandaigua_Info_Sheet_2010.pdf.

[24] P.L. 104-262, Veterans' Health Care Eligibility Reform Act of 1996, enacted 10/09/1996 (38 U.S.C. §7320).

[25] VA, VHA, *MIRECC of the VA Rocky Mountain Network (VISN 19 MIRECC)*, http: //www.mirecc.va.gov/ visn19http://www.mirecc.va.gov/visn19/index.asp.

[26] VA, VHA, VISN 19 MIRECC, *The Relationship Between Suicidal Ideation and Thinking Under Stress*, http://www.mirecc.va.gov/visn19/research/projects.asp.

[27] VA, VHA, VISN 19 MIRECC, Assessment of Cognitive Functioning as it Relates to Suicide Risk in Veterans with HIV/AIDS, http://www.mirecc.va.gov/visn19/research/projects.asp.

[28] Suicide prevention is a goal of the Mental Health Quality Enhancement Research Initiative (QUERI) within ORD. See VA Mental Health QUERI Center, *Strategic Plan*, December 2011, http://www.queri.research.va.gov/about/ strategic_plans/mh.pdf; and VA Mental Health QUERI Center, *Fact Sheet: Mental Health*, July 2014, http://www.queri.research.va.gov/about/ factsheets/mh_factsheet.pdf.

[29] The COE at Canandaigua evaluates implementation of suicide prevention initiatives.

[30] For example, the MIRECC of the VA Rocky Mountain Network is conducting a study to determine whether providing prescription medication in blister packages (rather than bottles) is associated with greater treatment adherence and fewer suicide-related overdoses among those at high risk of suicide. VA, VHA, *Blister Packaging Medications*, http://www.mirecc.va.gov/visn19/ research/projects.asp.

[31] *The War Within*, p. 13.

[32] U.S. Government Accountability Office, *VA Mental Health: Number of Veterans Receiving Care, Barriers Faced, and Efforts to Increase Access*, GAO-12-12, October 14, 2011, pp. 15-17, http://www.gao.gov/products/GAO-12-12.

[33] See for example VA, VHA, *Guide to VA Mental Health Services for Veterans & Families*, July 2012, http://www.mentalhealth.va.gov/docs/MHG_English.pdf; and VA, VHA, Office of Rural Health, *Mental Health Stigma: 10 Things You Should Know About*, http://www.ruralhealth.va.gov/ ruralclergytraining/10things/stigma.asp.

[34] Evelyn Chang and Alissa Simon, *Report on Integrating Mental Health Into PACT (IMHIP) in the VA*, VA Office of Patient Care Services, September 2013, http://www.hsrd.research.va.gov/ publications/internal/IMHIP-Report.pdf.

[35] VA, VHA, *Uniform Mental Health Services in VA Medical Centers and Clinics*, VHA Handbook 1160.01, September 11, 2008; and VA, VHA, *About VA Mental Health*, http://www.mentalhealth.va.gov/ vamentalhealthgroup.asp.

[36] VA, VHA, *Uniform Mental Health Services in VA Medical Centers and Clinics*, VHA Handbook 1160.01, September 11, 2008. In accordance with the Veterans Access, Choice, and Accountability Act of 2014 (P.L. 113-146), the VHA has established a wait-time goal (not specific to mental health) "to furnish care within 30 days of either the date that an appointment is deemed clinically appropriate by a VA health care provider, or if no such clinical determination has been made, the date a veteran prefers to be seen." Department of Veterans Affairs, "Expanded Access to Non-VA Care Through the Veterans Choice Program," 79 *Federal Register* 65571, November 5, 2014.

[37] See, for example, U.S. Congress, Senate Committee on Veterans' Affairs, *VA Mental Health Care: Ensuring Timely Access to High-Quality Care*, 113th Cong., 1st sess., March 20, 2013; U.S. Congress, House Committee on Veterans' Affairs, Subcommittee on Health, *Service Should Not Lead to Suicide: Access to VA's Mental Health Care*, 113th Cong., 2nd sess., July 10, 2014; and U.S. Congress, Senate Committee on Veterans' Affairs, *Mental Health and Suicide Among Veterans*, 113th Cong., 2nd sess., November 19, 2014.

[38] Meghan Hoyer and Tom Vanden Brook, "New data show long wait times remain at many VA hospitals," *USA Today*, November 16, 2014.

[39] *VHA Mental Health Program Evaluation*; and VHA, 2013 U.S. Department of Veterans Affairs National Mental Health Provider Survey, http://www.hospitalcompare.va.gov/.

[40] *The War Within*, p. 119.

[41] VA, VHA, *Programs for Veterans with Post-Traumatic Stress Disorder (PTSD)*, VHA Handbook 1160.03, March 12, 2010, p. 5, http://www.va.gov/vhapublications/View Publication. asp?pub_ID=2174.

[42] *VHA Mental Health Program Evaluation*, p. 153.

[43] *VHA Mental Health Program Evaluation*. For example, among veterans for whom maintenance medication is recommended, less than one-third received the recommended continuous treatment (p. 160). Similarly, among veterans receiving psychotherapy, "most did not include elements of an evidence-based modality" (p. 154).

[44] *VHA Mental Health Program Evaluation*. Less than two-thirds of veterans in a new treatment episode "have a documented assessment of their housing and employment needs" (p. 161). Among veterans with major depressive disorder who were receiving psychotherapy, less than a quarter (23%) "had documentation of an assessment of response to psychotherapy" (p. 155).

[45] VA, Office of Inspector General, *Healthcare Inspection: Evaluation of Suicide Prevention Program Implementation in VHA Facilities, January–June 2009*, Report No. 09-00326-223, Washington, DC, September 22, 2009; and VA, Office of Inspector General, *Combined Assessment Program Summary Report: Re-Evaluation of Suicide Safety Plan Practices in Veterans Health Administration Facilities*, Report No. 11-01380-128, Washington, DC, March 22, 2011.

[46] Department of Defense Task Force on the Prevention of Suicide by Members of the Armed Forces, *The Challenge and the Promise: Strengthening the Force, Preventing Suicide, and Saving Lives*, August 2010, pp. 55, 89, http://www.sprc.org/library_resources/items /challenge-and-promise-strengthening-force-preventing-suicide-andsaving-live; hereinafter referred to as *The Challenge and the Promise*.

[47] VA, VHA and Department of Health and Human Services (HHS), Substance Abuse and Mental Health Services Administration (SAMHSA), *Veterans Crisis Line*, http://www. veteranscrisisline.net/.

[48] HHS, SAMHSA, *National Suicide Prevention Lifeline*, http://www.suicidepreventionlifeline. org/.

[49] VA, VHA and HHS, SAMHSA, *About the Veterans Crisis Line*, http://www.veteranscrisisline. net/About/ AboutVeteransCrisisLine.aspx.

[50] J. John Mann et al., "Suicide Prevention Strategies: A Systematic Review," *Journal of the American Medical Association*, vol. 294, no. 16 (October 26, 2005), pp. 2064-2074.

[51] VA, VHA, *Mandatory Suicide Risk and Intervention Training for VHA Health Care Providers*, VHA Directive 1071, June 27, 2014, http://www.va.gov/vhapublications/ ViewPublication. asp?pub_ID=3011.

[52] VA, VHA, Office of Patient Care Services, Office of Mental Health Services, *Fact Sheet: VA Suicide Prevention Program*, March 2012, http://www.visn20.med.va.gov/VISN20/docs/ Suicide PreventionFactSheet32312.pdf.

[53] Mechanism of injury for suicides among the general U.S. population in CY2007 identified from Centers for Disease Control and Prevention, National Center for Health Statistics. *Compressed Mortality File 1999-2007. CDC WONDER On-line Database, compiled from Compressed Mortality File 1999-2007 Series 20 No. 2M, 2010*, http://wonder.cdc.gov/cmf-icd10.html.

[54] Marco Sarchiapone et al., "Controlling Access to Suicide Means," *International Journal of Environmental Research and Public Health*, vol. 8, no. 12 (2011), pp. 4550-4562; and Paul S.F. Yip et al., "Suicide 3: Means Restriction for Suicide Prevention," *The Lancet*, vol. 379, no. 9834 (2012), pp. 2393-2399.

[55] VA, VHA, *Health Awareness Campaigns: Gun Safety*, http://www.womens health.va. gov/ WOMENSHEALTH/outreachmaterials/safety/gunsafety.asp; and Caitlin Thompson, *Gun safety: An important conversation during Suicide Prevention Month*, VA, VHA, September

30, 2014, http://www.blogs.va.gov/VAntage/15434/gun-safety-an-importantconversation-during-suicide-prevention-month/.

[56] For example, the MIRECC of the VA Rocky Mountain Network is conducting a study to determine whether providing prescription medication in blister packages (rather than bottles) is associated with greater treatment adherence and fewer suicide-related overdoses among those at high risk of suicide. VA, VHA, *Blister Packaging Medications*, http://www.mirecc.va.gov/visn19/research/ projects.asp.

[57] *Charting the Future*, p. 11.

[58] See, for example, U.S. Congress, House Committee on Veterans' Affairs, Subcommittee on Health, *Service Should Not Lead to Suicide: Access to VA's Mental Health Care*, 113th Cong., 2nd sess., July 10, 2014; and U.S. Congress, Senate Committee on Veterans' Affairs, *Ensuring Veterans Receive the Care They Deserve—Addressing VA Mental Health Program Management*, 113th Cong., 2nd sess., November 19, 2014.

[59] Katherine E. Watkins and Harold Alan Pincus, *Veterans Health Administration Mental Health Program Evaluation: Capstone Report*, Altarum Institute and RAND Health, 2011, p. 153; hereinafter referred to as *VHA Mental Health Program Evaluation*.

[60] Margaret Harrell and Nancy Berglass, *Losing the Battle: The Challenge of Military Suicide*, Center for a New American Security (CNAS), Washington, DC, October 2011, p. 9; hereinafter referred to as *Losing the Battle*. CNAS is a 501(c)3 tax-exempt nonprofit organization that describes itself as independent and non-partisan. See http://www.cnas.org/about.

[61] See for example Stefan Timmermans, "Suicide determination and the professional authority of medical examiners.," *American Sociological Review*, vol. 70, no. 2 (2005), pp. 311-333; Hugh P. Whitt, "Where did the bodies go? The social construction of suicide data, New York City, 1976-1992," *Sociological Inquiry*, vol. 76, no. 2 (2006), pp. 166- 187; M.J. Breiding and B. Wiersema, "Variability of undetermined manner of death classification in the U.S.," *Injury Prevention*, vol. 12(Suppl II) (2006), pp. ii49-ii54.

[62] U.S. Government Accountability Office, VA Health Care: Improvements Needed in Monitoring Antidepressant Use for Major Depressive Disorder and in Increasing Accuracy of Suicide Data, GAO-15-55, December 12, 2014, http://www.gao.gov/products/GAO-15-55.

[63] The enrollment file includes veterans receiving benefits from the Veterans Benefits Administration, even if the veterans are not receiving care from VHA. VA researchers conducting a one-time study (not ongoing surveillance) combined information from the National Death Index with information from the DOD's Defense Manpower Data Center (DMDC) to identify suicides among veterans regardless of VA enrollment. The study was limited to veterans who served in Operations Enduring Freedom and/or Iraqi Freedom and who were separated alive from active duty between October 2001 and December 2005. See Han K. Kang and Tim A. Bullman, "Letter: Risk of Suicide Among US Veterans After Returning From the Iraq or Afghanistan War Zones," *Journal of the American Medical Association*, vol. 300, no. 6 (2008), pp. 652-653.

[64] *Charting the Future*, p. 40.

[65] *Losing the Battle*, p. 9; and *Charting the Future*, p. 40.

[66] *Losing the Battle*, p. 9.

[67] *Charting the Future*, p. 40.

[68] *Losing the Battle*, p.9.

[69] See CRS Report R43704, *Veterans Access, Choice, and Accountability Act of 2014 (H.R. 3230; P.L. 113-146).*

[70] Department of Veterans Affairs, "Expanded Access to Non-VA Care Through the Veterans Choice Program," 79 *Federal Register* 65571, November 5, 2014.

[71] *VHA Mental Health Program Evaluation*. For example, among veterans for whom maintenance medication is recommended, less than one-third received the recommended continuous treatment (p. 160). Similarly, among veterans receiving psychotherapy, "most did not include elements of an evidence-based modality" (p. 154).

[72] VA, VHA and DOD, *VA/DOD Clinical Practice Guidelines*, http://www.healthquality.va.gov/.

[73] The three study criteria were as follows: (1) providers reported having been trained in an evidenced-based therapy for posttraumatic stress disorder and major depressive disorder, (2) providers reported using evidence-based treatments for patients with those conditions, and (3) providers scored at least 15 on a 22-point scale of cultural competency with a military or veteran population. Terri Tanielian et al., *Ready to Serve: Community-Based Provider Capacity to Delivery Culturally Competent, Quality Mental Health Care to Veterans and Their Families*, The RAND Corporation, Santa Monica, CA, 2014.

[74] U.S. Congressional Budget Office, *Cost Estimate for H.R. 327 Joshua Omvig Veterans Suicide Prevention Act*, March 19, 2007; and U.S. Congressional Budget Office, *Cost Estimate for S.4797 Joshua Omvig Veterans Suicide Prevention Act*, July 10, 2007.

[75] U.S. Government Accountability Office, *Recovering Servicemembers: DOD and VA Have Jointly Developed the Majority of Required Policies but Challenges Remain*, GAO-09-728, July 2009, p. 25.

[76] Janet Kemp and Robert Bossarte, *Suicide Data Report, 2012*, VA, Mental Health Services, Suicide Prevention Program, February 1, 2013, http://www.va.gov/opa/docs/suicide-data-report-2012-final.pdf.

In: Major Depressive Disorder in Veterans ISBN: 978-1-63482-561-0
Editor: Casey P. Barton

Chapter 2

STATEMENT OF DR. HAROLD KUDLER, CHIEF MENTAL HEALTH CONSULTANT, VETERANS HEALTH ADMINISTRATION. HEARING ON "MENTAL HEALTH AND SUICIDE AMONG VETERANS"*

Good morning, Chairman Sanders, Ranking Member Burr, and Members of the Committee. Thank you for the opportunity to discuss the provision of mental health care to Veterans, particularly those who are at risk for suicide. I am accompanied today by Dr. Dean Krahn, Deputy Director of Mental Health Operations and Dr. Caitlin

Thompson, Deputy Director of VHA Suicide Prevention. My written statement will provide a brief overview of VA's mental health care system and programs for suicide prevention.

MENTAL HEALTH CARE OVERVIEW

Since September 11, 2001, more than two million Servicemembers have deployed to Iraq or Afghanistan. Long deployments and intense combat conditions require comprehensive support for the emotional and mental health of Veterans and their families. Accordingly, VA continues to develop and

* This is an edited, reformatted and augmented version of a statement presented November 19, 2014 before the Senate Committee on Veterans Affairs.

expand its mental health system. The number of Veterans receiving specialized mental health treatment from VA has risen each year, from 927,052 in Fiscal Year (FY) 2006 to more than 1.4 million in FY 2013. We anticipate that VA's requirements for providing mental health care will continue to grow for a decade or more after current operational missions have come to an end. VA believes this increase is partly attributable to proactive screening to identify Veterans who may have symptoms of depression, posttraumatic stress disorder (PTSD), substance use disorder, or those who have experienced military sexual trauma. In addition, VA has partnered with the Department of Defense (DoD) to develop the VA/DoD Integrated Mental Health Strategy to advance a coordinated public health model to improve access, quality, effectiveness, and efficiency of mental health services for Servicemembers, National Guard and Reserve, Veterans, and their families. Among the President's 19 new executive actions to improve the mental health of Servicemembers, Veterans, and their families, announced on August 26 is a further enhancement of transition from DoD to VA and civilian health care by ensuring that all Servicemembers leaving the military who are receiving care for mental health conditions are automatically enrolled in the *inTransition* program. In this program, trained mental health professionals assist these Servicemembers through "warm handoffs" to new care teams in VA or in the community. Further, mental health medications prescribed by DoD clinicians will be carried over into VA care unless a specific safety or clinical reason to make a change is identified. Those Servicemembers with multiple, complex, severe conditions such as traumatic brain injury, psychological trauma, or other cognitive, psychological, or emotional disorders will benefit by development of a single, joint comprehensive care plan between DoD and VA providers.

VA has many entry points for VHA mental health care. These entry points include 150 medical centers, 820 Community Based Outpatient Clinics (CBOCs), 300 Vet Centers providing readjustment counseling, a Veterans Crisis Line, VA staff on college and university campuses, and other outreach efforts. To serve the growing number of Veterans seeking mental health care, VA has deployed significant resources and increases in staff toward mental health services. Since March 2012, and with support from the President's Executive Order's focus on increasing mental health staffing, VA has added 2,444 mental health full-time equivalent employees and hired over 900 peer specialists and apprentices. Under the President's executive actions, VA will pilot the expansion of peer support beyond traditional mental health settings into primary care clinics in order to better connect with Veterans wherever they seek care.

As of April 2014, VHA has 21,158 Mental Health full-time equivalent employees providing direct inpatient and outpatient mental health care. VA has expanded access to mental health services with longer clinic hours, telemental heath capability to deliver services, and standards that mandate immediate access to mental health services to Veterans in crisis. Starting in FY 2012, the Office of Mental Health Operations initiated site visits to every VHA healthcare system to review and facilitate compliance with VHA mental health policy. All healthcare systems were visited in FY 2012 and subsequently one third are being visited each year. Recommendations are made to address opportunities for improvement identified as part of the site visit process and progress is monitored by the Office of Mental Health Operations. In an effort to increase access to mental health care and reduce any stigma associated with seeking such care, VA has integrated mental health into primary care settings. From the beginning of FY 2008 through July 2014, VA has provided more than 4 million Primary Care-Mental Health Integration (PC-MHI) clinic visits to more than 1,016,000 unique patients. This improves access by bringing care closer to where the Veteran can most easily receive these services, and improves quality of care by increasing the coordination of all aspects of care, both physical and mental. In addition, a second round of VA Community Mental Health Summits has recently been completed at virtually all major VA facilities across the nation and analysis of feedback from VA and Community participants is underway. Based on 2013 Summit recommendations, Community Mental Health Points of Contact have been identified at every VA Medical Center and each 2014 Summit included featured presentations on best practices in support of military and Veteran families and in populating the National Resource Directory in order to enhance referral to VA and community resources across America for use by any Servicemember, Veteran, family member, referring clinician or other stakeholder.

VA has made deployment of evidence-based therapies a critical element of its approach to mental health care and offers a continuum of recovery-oriented, patient-centered services across outpatient, residential, and inpatient settings. State-of-the-art treatment, including both psychotherapies and biomedical treatments, are available for the full range of mental health problems, such as PTSD, substance use disorders, and suicidality. While VA is primarily focused on evidence-based treatments, we are also assessing complementary and alternative treatment methodologies that need further research, such as meditation and acupuncture in the care of PTSD. VA has trained over 6,100 VA mental health professionals to provide two of the most effective evidence-based psychotherapies for PTSD, Cognitive Processing Therapy and Prolonged Exposure Therapy, as indicated in the VA/DoD Clinical Practice Guideline for PTSD[1]. VA operates the National Center for PTSD, which guides a national PTSD mentoring program, working with every specialty PTSD program across the VA health care system. The Center has begun a PTSD consultation program for any VA practitioners (including primary care practitioners and Homeless Program coordinators) who request consultation regarding a Veteran in treatment with PTSD. So far, the consultation program has provided 1,818 consultations and triaged an additional 143 requests from the Suicide Risk Management Consultation Program.

We know that there have been issues with Veteran access. We take those concerns seriously and continue to work to address them. Receiving direct feedback from Veterans concerning their care is vitally important. During the fourth quarter of FY 2013, as part of VHA's effort to seek direct input from Veterans in understanding their perceptions regarding access to care, we conducted a survey of over 40,000 Veterans who were receiving mental health care These results, and other outreach to Veterans, aid us as we strive to improve the timeliness of appointments; reminders for appointments; accessibility, engagement, and responsiveness of clinicians; availability and agreement with clinician on desired treatment frequency; helpfulness of mental health treatment; and treatment with respect and dignity.

PROGRAMS AND RESOURCES FOR SUICIDE PREVENTION

Overall, Veterans are at higher risk for suicide than the general U.S. population, notably Veterans with PTSD, pain, sleep disorders, depression, and substance use disorders. VA recognizes that even one Veteran suicide is too many. We are committed to ensuring the safety of our Veterans, especially when they are in crisis. Our suicide prevention program is based on enhancing Veterans' access to high-quality mental health care and programs specifically designed to help prevent Veteran suicide.

In partnership with the Substance Abuse and Mental Health Services Administration's National Suicide Prevention Lifeline, the Veterans Crisis Line/Military Crisis Line (VCL/MCL) connects Veterans and Servicemembers in crisis and their families and friends with qualified, caring VA responders through a confidential toll-free hotline (1-800-273-TALK (8255), then press 1) that offers 24/7 emergency assistance. This August marked seven years since the establishment of the initial program, which was later rebranded to show its direct support for Servicemembers. It has expanded to include a chat service and texting option. As of June 2014, the VCL/MCL has rescued 39,000 actively suicidal Veterans. As of June 2014, VCL/MCL has received over 1,250,000 calls, over 175,000 chat connections, and over 24,000 texts; it has also made over 220,000 referrals to Suicide Prevention Coordinators (SPC). In accordance with the President's August 31, 2012, Executive Order titled, "Improving Access to Mental Health Services for Veterans, Service Members and Military Families," VA completed hiring and training of additional staff to increase the capacity of the VCL/MCL by 50 percent.

VA has a network of over 300 SPCs located at every VA medical center and the largest CBOCs throughout the country. Overall, SPCs facilitate implementation of suicide prevention strategies within their respective medical centers and clinics to help ensure that all appropriate measures are being taken to prevent suicide in the Veteran patient population, particularly Veterans identified as being at high risk for suicidal behavior, and the SPCs engage in outreach to other Veterans, family members, and community partners. SPCs receive follow-up consults from the VCL/MCL call responders after immediate needs are addressed and any needed rescue actions are made. SPCs are required to follow up on consults received from the VCL/MCL within one business day to ensure timely access to care for Veterans callers who need additional support, treatment, or other services, including enrollment into VA's health care system. SPCs also plan, develop, implement, and evaluate their facility's Suicide Prevention Program to ensure continual quality improvement and excellence in customer service. SPCs are responsible for implementing VA's *Operation S.A.V.E* (Signs of suicidal thinking, Ask the questions, Verify the experience with the Veteran, and Expedite or Escort to Help). This is a one-to-two hour in-person training program provided by VA SPCs to Veterans and those who serve Veterans to help prevent suicide. Suicide prevention training is provided for every new VHA employee during Employee Orientation. It has now been provided to staff within the Veterans Benefits Administration and, through the Presidents' new executive actions, training will be provided for volunteer tax preparers at over 200 tax assistance facilities through partnership between VA and the Treasury Department. Further, the President's new executive actions mandate that refresher courses and training updates be developed and delivered at regular intervals. Our goal is to increase mental health awareness wherever Veterans and their family members are present and to continuously enhance and expand our response to their needs.

SPCs participate in outreach activities, which remain critically important to VA's goals of reducing stigma for mental health issues and improving access to services for all Veterans. Examples include community suicide prevention training and other educational programs, exhibits, and material distribution; meetings with state and local suicide prevention groups; and suicide prevention work with Active Duty/National Guard and Reserve units as well as college campuses. To date, each SPC is required to complete five or more outreach activities in his or her local community each month.

Veterans may be at high risk for suicide for various reasons. Determination of suicide risk is always a clinical judgment made after an evaluation of risk factors (e.g., history of past suicide attempts, recent discharge from an inpatient mental health unit), protective factors, and the presence or absence of warning signs. VHA Handbook 1160.01, "Uniform Mental Health Services in VA Medical Centers and Clinics," requires inpatient care be available to all Veterans with acute mental health needs (including imminent danger of self harm), either in a VA medical center or at a nearby facility through a contract or sharing agreement.

To ensure that high-risk Veterans are being monitored appropriately, SPCs manage a Category I Patient Record Flag (PRF) with a corresponding High-Risk List. The primary purpose of the High Risk for Suicide PRF is to communicate, consistent with appropriate privacy protections, to VA staff that a Veteran is at high risk for suicide, and the presence of a flag should be considered when making treatment decisions. Once a Veteran is identified as high risk, the SPC ensures that weekly contact is made with the Veteran for at least the first month, and that continued follow-up is made, as clinically appropriate. The SPC works with the treatment team to ensure that patients identified as being at high risk for suicide receive follow-up for any missed mental health and substance abuse appointments at VA. Clinicians are required to initiate at least three attempts to contact Veterans on the High-Risk List who fail to appear for mental health appointments and ensure appropriate documentation. If attempts to contact the Veteran are unsuccessful, the SPC collaborates with the Veteran's treatment team to decide what further action is appropriate involving a range of options from continued outreach efforts to the Veteran and/or family members up to requesting local law enforcement perform a welfare check in person.

SPCs ensure that all Veterans identified as high risk for suicide have completed a safety plan that is documented in their medical record, and that the Veteran is provided a copy of his or her safety plan.

National suicide prevention outreach efforts continue to expand and include targeted efforts for Veterans, Servicemembers, families, and friends. VA has sponsored public service announcements, rebranded and optimized the VCL/MCL Web site for mobile access and viewing, and developed social and traditional media advertisements designed to inform Veterans and their families of VA's VCL/MCL resources including phone, online chat, and text services. September was National Suicide Prevention Month, and VA launched its new outreach campaign theme for this year, "The Power of 1," which emphasizes that just one person, one conversation, or one small act can make a big difference to a Veteran or Servicemember in crisis by offering hope and connections to confidential support and resources.

In addition, VA established an online Community Provider Toolkit[2] for individuals outside of VA who provide care to Veterans. This provides an important resource in the wake of the Veterans Access, Choice, and Accountability Act of 2014. This Web site features key tools to support the mental health services provided to Veterans including information on connecting with VA, understanding military culture and experience, and working with patients with a variety of mental health conditions. There is also a comprehensive Suicide Prevention Mini-Clinic that provides clinicians with easy access to useful Veteran-focused treatment tools, including assessment, training, and educational handouts.[3]

In 2010, DoD and VA approved plans for a Joint Suicide Data Repository (SDR) as a shared resource for improving our understanding of patterns and characteristics of suicide among Veterans and Servicemembers. The combined DoD and VA search of data available in the National Death Index represents the single largest mortality search of a population with a history of military service on record. The DoD/VA Joint SDR is overseen by the Defense Suicide Prevention Office and VA's Suicide Prevention Program.

On February 1, 2013, VA released a report on Veteran suicides including data from the SDR, a result of the most comprehensive review of Veteran suicide rates ever undertaken by VA. With assistance from state partners providing real-time data for SDR, VA is now better able to assess the effectiveness of its suicide prevention programs and identify specific populations that need targeted interventions. This new information will assist VA in identifying where at-risk Veterans may be located and improving the Department's ability to target specific suicide interventions and outreach activities in order to reach Veterans early and proactively. These data will also help VA continue to examine the effectiveness of suicide prevention programs being implemented in specific geographic locations (e.g., rural areas), as well as care settings, such as primary care, in order to replicate effective programs in other areas. VA continues to receive state data that are being included in the SDR. VA plans to update the suicide data report later this year.

In 2011, the most recent year for which national data are available, the age-adjusted rate of suicide in the U.S. general population was 12.32 per 100,000 persons per year. At just over 12 for every 100,000 U.S. residents, the 2011 rate of suicide has increased by approximately 15 percent since 2001. Rates of suicide in the United States are higher among males, middle-aged adults, residents in rural areas, and those with mental health conditions.

The most recent available data show that suicide rates are generally lower among Veterans who use VHA services than among Veterans who do not use VHA services. In 2011, the rate of suicide among those who use VHA services was 35.5 per 100,000 persons per year; a decrease of approximately 6 percent since 2001. Rates of suicide among those who use VHA services have remained relatively stable; ranging from 35.5 to 37.5 per 100,000 persons per year over the past 4 years. Despite evidence of increased risk among middle-aged adults (35-64 years) in the U.S. general population, rates of suicide among middle-aged adults who use VHA services have decreased by more than 16 percent between the years 1999-2010. For males without a history of using VHA services, the rate increased by more than 60 percent, whereas for males with a history of using VHA services, the rate decreased by more than 30 percent. Decreases in suicide rates and improvements in outcomes were also observed for some other high-risk groups. Between 2001 and 2010, rates of suicide decreased by more than 28 percent among VHA users with a mental health or substance abuse diagnosis, and the proportion of VHA users who die from suicide within 12 months of a survived suicide attempt has decreased by approximately 5 percent during the same time period.[4]

In response to these findings, VA has been focusing on public health and community programming. This includes increased and targeted outreach efforts throughout the country to Veterans and their family members with significant emphasis on safety. We encourage Veterans and their families to learn more about mental illness and to take precautions particularly during times of stress (e.g., properly storing weapons and medications). Being alert to items in the environment that offer potential means of suicidal behavior can make a life-saving difference during a crisis. Messaging and interventions are geared toward those who are most at risk for suicide, including our younger male Veterans, women Veterans, Veterans with mental health conditions, and established patients who are known to be at high risk for suicide. Strategies include specialized training for VHA staff to enhance their recognition and treatment of those at risk, and offering Veterans skills-building and other preventive strategies to address major stressors in their lives. Furthermore, VA is engaged in ongoing research to determine the most effective mental health treatments and suicide prevention strategies. Finally, VA has established the Mental Health Innovations Integrated Project Team that is working to implement early intervention strategies for specific high-risk groups including Veterans with PTSD, pain, sleep disorders, depression, and substance use disorders. Through early intervention, VA hopes to reduce the risk of suicide for Veterans in these high-risk groups.

Readjustment Counseling Service (RCS)

VA's RCS provides a wide range of readjustment counseling services to eligible Veterans and active duty Servicemembers who have served in combat zones and their families. RCS also provides comprehensive readjustment counseling for eligible Veterans and Servicemembers who experienced military sexual trauma, as well as offering bereavement counseling to immediate family members of Servicemembers who died while on active duty. These services are provided in a safe and confidential environment through a national network of 300 community-based Vet Centers located in all 50 states (as well as the District of Columbia, American Samoa, Guam, and Puerto Rico), 70 Mobile Vet Centers, and the Vet Center Combat Call Center (877-WAR-VETS or 877-927-8387). In FY 2013, Vet Centers provided over 1.5 million visits to Veterans, active duty Servicemembers, and their families. The Vet Center program has provided services to over 30 percent of Operation Enduring Freedom/Operation Iraqi Freedom/Operation New Dawn Veterans who have left active duty. A new executive action will promote awareness of Vet Centers for combat Veterans, Servicemembers, and their families through a new outreach campaign that partners VA with First Lady Michelle Obama and Dr. Jill Biden's Joining Forces initiative.

CLOSING STATEMENT

Mr. Chairman, VA is committed to providing timely, high quality care that our Veterans have earned and deserve, and we continue to take every available action and create new opportunities to improve suicide prevention services. We appreciate the opportunity to appear before you today, and my colleagues and I are prepared to respond to any questions you may have.

End Notes

[1] http://www.healthquality.va.gov/guidelines/MH/ptsd/cpg PTSD-FULL-201011612.pdf
[2] http://www.mentalhealth.va.gov/communityproviders
[3] http://www.mentalhealth.va.gov/communityproviders/clinic suicideprevention.asp
[4] http://www.blogs.va.gov/VAntage/11973/january-2014-va-suicide-data-update/

In: Major Depressive Disorder in Veterans
Editor: Casey P. Barton
ISBN: 978-1-63482-561-0

Chapter 3

VA HEALTH CARE: IMPROVEMENTS NEEDED IN MONITORING ANTIDEPRESSANT USE FOR MAJOR DEPRESSIVE DISORDER AND IN INCREASING ACCURACY OF SUICIDE DATA*

United States Government Accountability Office

WHY GAO DID THIS STUDY

In 2013, VA estimated that about 1.5 million veterans required mental health care, including services for MDD. MDD is a debilitating mental illness related to reduced quality of life and productivity, and increased risk for suicide. VA also plays a role in suicide prevention. GAO was asked to review how VA tracks veterans prescribed antidepressants and what suicide data VA uses in its prevention efforts.

This report examines (1) VA's data on veterans with MDD, including those prescribed an antidepressant; (2) the extent that veterans with MDD who are prescribed antidepressants receive recommended care and the extent to which VA monitors such care; and (3) the quality of data VA requires VAMCs to collect on veteran suicides. GAO analyzed VA data, interviewed VA

---

* This is an edited, reformatted and augmented version of a United States Government Accountability Office publication, No. GAO-15-55, dated November 2014.

officials, and conducted site visits to six VAMCs selected based on geography and population served. From each of these six VAMCs, GAO also reviewed five randomly selected medical records for veterans diagnosed with MDD and prescribed an antidepressant in 2012, as well as all completed BHAP templates. The results cannot be generalized across VA but provide insights.

WHAT GAO RECOMMENDS

GAO recommends that VA identify and address MDD coding discrepancies; implement processes to review data and assess deviations from recommended care; and implement processes to improve completeness, accuracy, and consistency of veteran suicide data. VA concurred with GAO's recommendations and described its plans to implement them.

WHAT GAO FOUND

GAO's analysis of Department of Veterans Affairs (VA) data for fiscal years 2009 through 2013 shows that about 10 percent of veterans who received VA health care services were diagnosed with major depressive disorder (MDD). MDD is characterized by depressed mood or loss of interest along with other symptoms for 2 weeks or more that represent a change in the way individuals function from their previous behaviors. Because GAO found diagnostic coding discrepancies in 11 of the 30 veterans' medical records it reviewed from six VA medical centers (VAMC), VA's data may understate the prevalence of MDD among veterans being treated through VA, to the extent that such discrepancies may permeate VA's data. One treatment for MDD is the use of medications such as antidepressants. According to GAO's analysis, 94 percent of veterans diagnosed with MDD were prescribed at least one antidepressant.

VA policy states that antidepressant treatment must be consistent with VA's current clinical practice guideline (CPG); however, GAO's review of 30 veterans' medical records identified deviations from selected MDD CPG recommendations for most veterans reviewed. For example, 26 of the 30 veterans were not assessed using a standardized assessment tool at 4 to 6 weeks after initiation of treatment, as recommended in the CPG. Additionally, 10 veterans did not receive follow up within the time frame recommended in the CPG. GAO found that VA does not have a system-wide process in place to identify and fully assess whether the care provided is consistent with the CPG. As a result, VA does not know the extent to which veterans with MDD who have been prescribed antidepressants are receiving care as recommended in the CPG and whether appropriate actions are taken by VAMCs to mitigate potentially significant risks to veterans.

The demographic and clinical data that VA collects on veteran suicides were not always complete, accurate, or consistent. VA's Behavioral Health Autopsy Program (BHAP) is a quality initiative to improve VA's suicide prevention efforts by identifying information that VA can use to develop policy and procedures to help prevent future suicides. The BHAP templates are a mechanism by which VA collects suicide data from VAMC's review of veteran medical records. GAO's review of 63 BHAP templates at five VAMCs found that 40 of the templates that VAMCs submitted to VA Central Office had incomplete data. Also, GAO found that the BHAP templates VAMCs submitted contained inaccurate data. For example, 6 BHAP templates included a date of death that was incorrect based on information in the veteran's medical record, and 9 BHAP templates included an incorrect number of outpatient VA mental health visits in the last 30 days. Moreover, GAO found that VAMCs submitted inconsistent information because they interpreted VA's guidance on completing the BHAP templates differently. This situation was further exacerbated because BHAP templates prepared by VAMCs are generally not being reviewed at any level within the Department for completeness, accuracy, and consistency. Lack of complete, accurate, and consistent data and poor oversight can inhibit VA's ability to identify, evaluate, and improve ways to better inform its suicide prevention efforts.

ABBREVIATIONS

BHAP	Behavioral Health Autopsy Program
BHL	Behavioral Health Laboratory
CPG	clinical practice guideline
DOD	Department of Defense
Handbook	*Uniform Mental Health Services in VA Medical Centers and Clinics* handbook
MDD	major depressive disorder
OIG	Office of Inspector General
OMHO	Office of Mental Health Operations

OMHS	Office of Mental Health Services
PHQ	Patient Health Questionnaire
SPAN	Suicide Prevention Application Network
TIDES	Translating Initiatives for Depression into Effective Solutions
VA	Department of Veterans Affairs
VAMC	Veterans Affairs medical center
VISN	Veterans Integrated Service Network

* * *

November 12, 2014

The Honorable Mike Coffman
Chairman
Subcommittee on Oversight and Investigations
Committee on Veterans' Affairs
House of Representatives

Dear Mr. Chairman:

In 2013, the Department of Veterans Affairs (VA) estimated that about 1.5 million veterans required mental health services, which VA provides in a variety of settings, including VA medical centers (VAMC), community-based outpatient clinics, and residential treatment programs.[1] Mental health treatment includes services for depression—a mood disorder that causes a persistent feeling of sadness and loss of interest. One type of depression, major depressive disorder (MDD), is a particularly debilitating mental illness and is associated with reduced quality of life, reduced productivity, and increased risk for suicide. These negative effects underscore the importance of timely, evidence-based assessment for and treatment of MDD, which may include medications, such as antidepressants, psychotherapy, or a combination of both. Treatment of veterans with MDD can improve their occupational and social functioning and their overall well-being.

In addition to providing ongoing care to veterans with MDD, VA plays a role in suicide risk assessment and prevention among veterans. According to VA, about one-quarter of the 18 to 22 veterans who die by suicide each day were receiving care through VA. 2 Research has identified numerous risk factors for suicide among veterans, which include substance use disorder, physical impairments, previous suicide attempts, and depression. Additionally, life stressors, such as marital or financial problems, contribute to a veteran's risk of suicide.

Given the debilitating effects of depression, VA's monitoring of veterans with MDD is critical to ensuring positive health outcomes. Additionally, the relatively high veteran suicide rate makes it important that VA effectively employs data related to suicides in its prevention efforts. You asked us to review how VA tracks and manages veterans prescribed antidepressants and what suicide data VA uses in its suicide prevention efforts. In this report, we examine

1) the data VA has on veterans with MDD, including the extent to which they were prescribed antidepressants;
2) the extent to which veterans with MDD who are prescribed an antidepressant receive recommended care and the extent to which VA monitors such care; and
3) the information VA requires VAMCs to collect on veteran suicides.

To examine the data VA has on veterans with MDD, including the extent to which veterans were prescribed antidepressants, we analyzed national VA data from fiscal years 2009 through 2013 and interviewed VA officials.[3] The data we analyzed included information on veterans' demographic characteristics, health care services, and medications provided through VA.[4] We considered a veteran to have MDD if, in at least one fiscal year included in our review, the veteran had two or more outpatient encounters or at least one inpatient hospital stay associated with a diagnosis of MDD.[5] To ensure the reliability of the data we analyzed, we interviewed VA Central Office officials, reviewed relevant documentation and veterans' medical records, and conducted electronic testing to identify missing data and obvious errors.[6] On the basis of these activities, we determined that the data we analyzed were sufficiently reliable for our purposes. We also conducted site visits to 6 of the 150 VAMCs selected for variation in complexity of health care services offered, geographic location, and number of veterans using mental health services. These six VAMCs were located in Canandaigua, New York; Gainesville, Florida; Iowa City, Iowa; Philadelphia, Pennsylvania; Phoenix, Arizona; and Reno, Nevada.[7] At each site, we interviewed VAMC staff about the data maintained on veterans diagnosed with MDD. In addition, we reviewed a random, nongeneralizeable sample of medical records for five veterans treated at each of the six VAMCs for a total of 30 veterans. We selected veterans for review that were diagnosed with MDD and had a new treatment episode of an antidepressant in calendar year 2012. Starting with the initial encounter in 2012 that was associated with the new antidepressant prescription, we reviewed the medical records to determine if the diagnostic code entered for subsequent encounters was consistent with a diagnosis of MDD.

To analyze the extent to which VA monitors whether veterans with MDD who are prescribed an antidepressant receive care as recommended by VA's clinical practice guideline (CPG) for MDD, we reviewed VA policy documents and interviewed VA Central Office officials responsible for developing and implementing VA mental health policy. 8 We identified the oversight processes VA has in place to monitor the recommendations in the CPG and assessed whether this oversight provides VA with adequate information to identify nonconformance with recommended practices, assess the risk, and address nonconformance, as appropriate. We selected three CPG recommendations for inclusion in our review that had among the highest strength of research evidence, were sufficiently specific to enable us to determine the extent to which VA providers were following the recommendation, and would not require clinical judgment to determine the extent to which VA providers were following the recommendation.[9] To examine how the recommendations we selected were implemented, we reviewed the 30 medical records from our selected six VAMCs to assess the extent to which the antidepressant treatment-related care VAMCs provided was consistent with the CPG recommendations. We also interviewed VAMC officials regarding the care provided to veterans with MDD prescribed an antidepressant. Results from our 30 medical record reviews cannot be generalized to the VAMC visited or other VAMCs.

To analyze the information VA requires VAMCs to collect on veteran suicides, we reviewed VA policies, guidance, and documents related to VA's suicide prevention efforts to identify the data collected by VA staff on veteran suicides. We also interviewed VA Central Office and other officials responsible for VA's suicide prevention program. Additionally, through the site visits to six VAMCs, we obtained documents and interviewed officials regarding the collection of veteran suicide data and suicide prevention initiatives. We compared 63 data templates related to veteran suicides completed by VAMC staff as of the date of our site visits—or the date of our request for virtual site visits—to information included in the veterans' medical records and to templates we received from VA Central Office. [10] We identified fields in the documents to review based on whether the field related to aspects of VA treatment—including treatment for mental health conditions—and the date of the veteran's death. We identified these fields because they did not require clinical judgment to assess. Results from our review of veteran suicide data can be generalized to the VAMCs we visited, but cannot be generalized to other VAMCs. We also interviewed relevant staff of the six Veterans Integrated Service Networks (VISN), or regional networks of care, for the sites we visited to obtain information on suicide prevention efforts in that VISN.[11]

For more information on our scope and methodology, see appendix I.

We conducted this performance audit from November 2013 to November 2014 in accordance with generally accepted government auditing standards. Those standards require that we plan and perform the audit to obtain sufficient, appropriate evidence to provide a reasonable basis for our findings and conclusions based on our audit objectives. We believe that the evidence obtained provides a reasonable basis for our findings and conclusions based on our audit objectives.

BACKGROUND

VA provides care to veterans with mental health needs through its 150 VAMCs, which may include both specialty mental health care settings—including mental health clinics—and other settings that may provide mental health services but focus primarily on other types of care, such as primary care. VA has implemented a program to co-locate mental health care providers within primary care settings in an effort to promote effective treatment of common mental health conditions in the primary care environment while allowing mental health specialists to focus on veterans with more severe mental illnesses.

Care for Veterans with MDD

According to VA, the prevalence of MDD in primary care settings among veterans being treated through VA is higher than that among the general population. MDD is characterized by the presence of depressed mood or loss of interest or pleasure along with other symptoms for a period of at least 2 weeks that represent a change in previous functioning.[12] VA has policies and guidance in place related to treating veterans with MDD. For example, the *Uniform Mental Health Services in VA Medical Centers and Clinics* handbook (Handbook), which defines VA's minimum clinical requirements for mental health services, requires that VA facilities provide evidence-based treatment through the administration of medication, when indicated, consistent with the MDD CPG.[13] The CPG is guidance intended by VA to reduce current practice variation between clinicians and provide facilities with a structured framework to help improve patient outcomes.[14]

The MDD CPG provides evidence-based recommendations as guidance for clinicians who provide care for veterans with MDD.[15] The MDD CPG includes approximately 200 recommendations to provide information and assist in decision making for clinicians who provide care for adults with MDD.[16] For example, the CPG recommends that standardized assessments of depressive symptoms, such as the nine item Patient Health Questionnaire (PHQ-9), should be used at the initial assessment of MDD symptoms, to monitor treatment response at 4-6 weeks after initiation of treatment, after each change in treatment, and periodically thereafter until full remission is achieved.[17] Evidence shows that follow-up assessment is effective 4-6 weeks after initiation of treatment, making timely follow-up visits an important part of clinicians' ability to assess whether the current treatment plan is effective or should be modified. According to the MDD CPG, veterans with MDD treated with antidepressants should be closely observed, particularly at the beginning of treatment and following dosage changes, to maximize veterans' recovery and to mitigate any negative treatment effects, including worsening of depressive symptoms. The CPG should not take the place of the clinician's clinical judgment.

VA Suicide Prevention Efforts

Beginning in June 2006, VA implemented several initiatives aimed at suicide prevention, including appointing a National Suicide Prevention Coordinator, developing data systems to increase understanding of suicide among veterans and inform VA suicide prevention programs, and instituting suicide prevention programs in VAMCs throughout the country. Additionally, VA Central Office established the Center of Excellence for Suicide Prevention and the Veterans Crisis Line in 2007. The Center of Excellence collects VA suicide prevention program data, which provides information on veteran suicide completions and suicide attempts for veterans receiving VA care, as well as those veterans not receiving VA care. VA's Veterans Crisis Line provides toll-free, confidential support 24 hours per day for veterans, their families, and their friends through phone, online chat, or text message.[18] In fiscal year 2013, the Veterans Crisis Line fielded approximately 287,000 calls, 54,800 online chats, and 11,300 text messages.

As part of VAMCs' suicide prevention programs, the Handbook requires each VAMC to have a suicide prevention coordinator whose responsibilities include

- establishing and maintaining a list of veterans assessed to be at high risk for suicide;
- monitoring these high-risk veterans;
- responding to referrals from staff and the Veterans Crisis Line;
- collaborating with community organizations and partners;
- training staff members who have contact with veterans at the VAMC, community organizations, and partners; and
- collecting and reporting information on veterans who die by suicide and who attempt suicide.

See appendix II for more information on VAMCs' tracking of veterans at high risk for suicide.

VA Suicide Data

VA Central Office uses several mechanisms to collect data on veteran suicides to help improve its suicide prevention efforts. One such mechanism includes data submitted by suicide prevention coordinators at VAMCs on known veterans who die by suicide.[19] Beginning in December 2012, VA Central Office began a national initiative to collect demographic, clinical, and other related information on veteran suicides as a quality improvement initiative to improve its suicide prevention efforts by identifying information that can be used by VA Central Office to develop policy and procedures to help prevent future veteran deaths.[20] This initiative, the Behavioral Health Autopsy Program (BHAP), replaced previous VA Central Office requirements to collect data on completed suicides.[21] VA Central Office officials explained that they transitioned to the BHAP initiative to collect more systematic and comprehensive information about suicides, to incorporate interviews of family members of those who die by suicide, and to collect more contextual information.

According to VA, the BHAP quality initiative has been adapted from a traditional psychological autopsy research framework that emphasizes the importance of information from outside sources as well as from those within the health care setting. The BHAP initiative is being implemented by VA in four phases:

- **Phase 1—Standardized chart reviews**: VAMCs' suicide prevention coordinators are required to complete standardized chart reviews for all veterans' suicides known to VAMC staff and reported on or after October 1, 2012.[22] These reviews include specific information on a veteran's utilization of VA health care services, as well as a veteran's mental health diagnoses and risk factors for suicide. VA Central Office has instructed suicide prevention coordinators to use all available information, including VA medical records and information from a veteran's family members to complete the chart review. These reviews are submitted to VA Central Office through completion of a BHAP Post-Mortem Chart Analysis Template (BHAP template) and VA Central Office has provided suicide prevention coordinators with a BHAP Guide on how to complete the fields in the BHAP template. VA Central Office requires VAMCs to submit the BHAP template within 30 days of VAMC staff becoming aware of a veteran's death by suicide.
- **Phase 2—Interviews with family members**: In fiscal year 2013, VA Central Office began conducting interviews with family members of veterans who have died by suicide to obtain information on suicide risks, barriers to care, and suggestions for new programs to prevent suicide.[23]
- **Phase 3—Clinician questionnaire**: This phase, which has not yet been implemented, will include an interview with the last provider that saw the veteran prior to his or her death. VA officials stated that there are no plans to begin this phase within calendar year 2014, and they have not established a future time table for implementing this phase.
- **Phase 4—Public record review**: This phase, which has also not been implemented, will be used to locate public records to identify stressors in the veteran's life, such as a bankruptcy or divorce. Officials stated that there are no plans to begin this phase within calendar year 2014, and they have not established a future time table for implementing this phase.

Since beginning the BHAP initiative, VA Central Office has internally issued two interim reports on data and trends from the submitted BHAP templates as part of Phase 1. The reports include information for veterans who died by suicide, both with and without a history of VA health care service utilization. Analyses of data on demographic characteristics, case information, period of service, and risk and protective factors were included for all veterans. Data on clinical characteristics and indicators of increased risk at the time of the veteran's last contact with a VA provider were limited to veterans that utilized VA health care services.

In addition to the BHAP initiative, VA also requires VAMCs to collect and submit data on suicide attempts and completions through the following mechanisms.[24]

- **Suicide Prevention Application Network (SPAN)**: Through SPAN, VAMCs submit information to VA Central Office on the number of veterans that completed suicide, the number of suicide attempts, and indicators of suicide prevention efforts, such as outreach events conducted each month by suicide prevention coordinators.
- **Suicide behavior reports**: VAMC clinicians must complete a suicide behavior report when they learn that a veteran attempted or completed suicide and add that report to the respective veteran's medical record. This report includes the date and time of the event, and other observations related to the suicide attempt or completed suicide. According to VA policy, information from suicide behavior reports is used for National Patient Safety reporting requirements and to populate SPAN.
- **Root cause analyses**: Patient safety managers at VAMCs complete root cause analyses for suicide attempts and completed suicides under certain circumstances, such as when the attempt occurs at the VAMC during an inpatient stay or within 72 hours of being discharged from inpatient care. Root cause analyses are used to identify the factors that contributed to adverse events or close calls and any steps VAMCs could implement to prevent similar events in the future.

See appendix III for how VAMC and VISN officials we interviewed told us they have utilized data related to suicides and suicide behavior.

VA Data Show That 10 Percent of Veterans Had MDD and Most Were Prescribed at Least One Antidepressant, but VA Data May Underestimate MDD Prevalence

Data for fiscal years 2009 through 2013 show that about 10 percent of veterans who received health care services through VA were diagnosed with MDD, and of those, 94 percent were prescribed an antidepressant. However, due to diagnostic coding discrepancies we found in a sample of veterans' medical records, VA's data may not accurately reflect the prevalence of MDD among veterans.

VA Data Show About 10 Percent of Veterans Had a Diagnosis of MDD, and Almost All Were Prescribed at Least One Antidepressant

Based on our analysis of VA data from veterans' medical records and administrative sources, 532,222 veterans—about 10 percent of veterans who received health care services through VA[25]—had a diagnosis of MDD from fiscal years 2009 through 2013. Among those veterans, the majority (60 percent) were 35 to 64 years of age. Most (86 percent) were not veterans of the recent conflicts in Iraq and Afghanistan.[26] In addition, most of these veterans were male (87 percent) and the highest proportion was white (68 percent) and non-Hispanic (87 percent). See table 1 for a summary of characteristics of veterans who had a diagnosis of MDD from fiscal years 2009 through 2013.

We also found that about 499,000 of the 532,222 (94 percent) veterans who had a diagnosis of MDD from fiscal years 2009 through 2013 were prescribed at least one antidepressant. Of those veterans, the majority (about 73 percent) were dispensed a 12-week supply of an antidepressant at the start of an MDD episode. Fewer veterans (about 58 percent) were dispensed a 6-month supply of an antidepressant over the course of their treatment. Receiving a 12-week supply of an antidepressant can be important for addressing depressive symptoms initially, while continued treatment after remission of depressive symptoms, such as receiving a 6-month supply of an antidepressant, is associated with a decreased risk of relapse, according to the CPG.

Table 1. Characteristics of Veterans Who Received Health Care through the Department of Veterans Affairs and had a Diagnosis of Major Depressive Disorder, Fiscal Years 2009-2013

Veteran characteristics	Number of veterans with major depressive disorder	Percentage of veterans with major depressive disorder
Age		
18-24	3,347	0.6
25-34	54,054	10.2
35-44	57,458	10.8
45-54	96,321	18.1
55-64	164,640	30.9
65-74	115,358	21.7
75+	41,044	7.7
Era of service		
Recent conflicts in Iraq & Afghanistan[a]	75,934	14.3
All other eras	456,288	85.7
Sex		
Male	460,660	86.6
Female	71,562	13.5
Race		
White	361,921	68.0
Black	96,511	18.1
Asian & Pacific Islander	7,098	1.3
Native American	3,484	0.7
Other[b]	23,375	4.4
Not Identified	14,727	2.8
Missing Information	25,106	4.7
Ethnicity		
Non-Hispanic	465,448	87.5
Hispanic	38,577	7.3
Not Identified	14,438	2.7
Missing Information	13,759	2.6

Source: GAO analysis of Department of Veterans Affairs and Department of Defense data. | GAO-15-55

Notes: N=532,222 veterans. Percentages may not equal 100 due to rounding.

[a]These conflicts include Operation Iraqi Freedom, Operation Enduring Freedom, and Operation New Dawn.

[b]This category includes veterans who identified themselves as Hispanic or multiple race.

VA's Data May Not Fully Reflect the Extent to Which Veterans Have MDD Due to a Lack of Diagnostic Coding Precision by Clinicians

Based on our review of the documentation in 30 veterans' medical records from VA's medical record system, we found that over one-third (11) had diagnostic coding discrepancies. Specifically, these 11 veterans had at least one encounter where the clinician documented a diagnosis of MDD in the veteran's medical record, but the clinician did not code the encounter accordingly. Instead, the clinician coded the encounter as "depression not otherwise specified," a less specific code.[27] According to the fourth edition of the *Diagnostic and Statistical Manual of Mental Disorders*, depression not otherwise specified is to be used to code disorders with depressive features that do not meet criteria for MDD and other depressive disorders,[28] or to indicate depressive symptoms about which there is inadequate or contradictory information.[29] VA's data on the number of veterans with MDD are based on the diagnostic codes associated with patient encounters, so the discrepancies we found indicate that the number of veterans with MDD is most likely not fully reflected in these data. Accurately identifying the veteran population with MDD is critical to assessing Department performance in treating veterans in accordance with the MDD CPG and measuring health outcomes for these veterans. VA Central Office reviewed the 11 medical records where we found coding discrepancies and agreed that the encounters were not coded accurately. According to a VA Central Office official, the encounters we identified were corrected in the veterans' medical record.

According to VHA Handbook 1907.03 - *Health Information Management Clinical Coding Program Procedures*, VAMCs are required to monitor the accuracy of coding and provide training as necessary in order to help ensure accurate coding. VAMC officials from all six sites in our review said that monthly or quarterly coding audits are conducted at their facilities and the findings of those audits are reviewed and action is taken to correct issues with the accuracy and reliability of coding. However, at five of the six VAMCs in our review, those audits focus on billable encounters—that is, encounters that are billed to a third party, such as private health insurance plans—in part because of the potential opportunity for facilities to collect third-party revenue from these encounters.[30] Among the 11 veterans' medical records where we identified coding discrepancies, all of the discrepancies were associated with outpatient, nonbillable encounters, the coding of which, according to a VA Central Office official, is not typically conducted by VAMC medical coders—

staff who are trained specifically in medical coding terminology and standards and are responsible for coding inpatient admissions and discharges—or subject to coding audits.

Diagnostic coding in VA's medical record system for outpatient encounters is typically performed by clinicians. VISN officials and VA medical center clinicians we interviewed said that clinicians do not place a lot of importance on selecting a more precise diagnostic code because it does not significantly change the patient care that is provided or the type of treatment prescribed. In addition, in the interest of expediency, clinicians may select a previously used or frequently used diagnostic code for depression rather than take the time to search for a more precise code. For example, within the medical record, clinicians may access a list of previous or current diagnoses applicable to the veteran (commonly referred to as the "problem list") or a list of frequently used diagnostic codes in the facility. According to VISN and VAMC officials, the problem list is not typically kept up to date by clinicians and as a result, MDD may not be listed and readily available for clinicians to select. As a result of our review, VA Central Office officials reported that they had discovered a software mapping error in VA's medical record system where the selection of MDD as a diagnosis when using a keyword search function may result in the selection of the depression not otherwise specified diagnostic code by mistake.[31] Officials stated that they anticipate that the software error—which applies to all VAMCs—would be fixed by November 2014. Officials also stated that the solution would apply only to those encounters coded from that point going forward and would not retroactively correct any coding discrepancies that may have occurred before the error was addressed. VA Central Office officials could not tell us if any of the 11 coding discrepancies that we identified were a result of this software error.

Officials at most of the six VISNs we spoke with do not conduct reviews of medical coding done by clinicians. However, as a result of our inquiry, one VISN we interviewed reported in the late spring of 2014 that it had extracted data on MDD-related encounters and noticed the high use of depression not otherwise specified coding for the facilities within its VISN, as well as all VAMCs nationwide. Officials from this VISN said the lack of coding specificity has implications for being able to accurately examine health outcomes related to the treatment of depression and that they are planning to further analyze encounter data within their VISN to determine the appropriateness of diagnostic coding based upon medical record documentation. As of September 2014, the VISN had not reported any additional steps to address this issue.

NOT ALL VETERANS IN OUR REVIEW RECEIVED CPG-RECOMMENDED CARE AND VA LACKS MECHANISMS TO DETERMINE WHETHER THIS CARE IS PROVIDED

Based on the three CPG recommendations we selected, veterans in our review with MDD who have been prescribed antidepressants did not always receive care as recommended in the MDD CPG. Additionally, VA does not know the extent to which veterans with MDD who have been prescribed antidepressants are receiving care as recommended in the CPG, and VA Central Office has not developed mechanisms to determine the extent to which mental health care delivery conforms to the recommendations in the MDD CPG.

Veterans We Reviewed Did Not Always Receive Care As Recommended

We found that almost all of the 30 veterans with MDD who have been prescribed antidepressants included in our review did not receive care in accordance with the three MDD CPG recommendations we reviewed. VA policy states that antidepressant treatment must be consistent with VA's current, evidence-based CPG.[32] However, VA Central Office mental health officials were unable to tell us what it means to provide care that is consistent with the CPG, because, while a veteran's treatment should be informed by the CPG recommendations, determining the extent to which the treatment is consistent with CPG recommendations would need to be done on a veteran-by-veteran basis. The CPG is intended to reduce practice variation and help improve patient outcomes, but without an understanding of the extent to which veterans are receiving care that is consistent with the CPG, VA may be unable to ensure that it meets the intent of the CPG and improves veteran health outcomes.

Through our review of 30 medical records from the six VAMCs we selected, we found examples of deviations from the CPG recommendations for almost all veterans in our review. 33 Table 2 below depicts the specific recommendations we reviewed and the number of veterans that did not receive care consistent with the corresponding CPG recommendation.

Table 2. Number of Veterans in GAO's Sample Not Receiving Care As Recommended in the Clinical Practice Guideline (CPG) for Major Depressive Disorder (MDD)

CPG recommendation	Number of veterans not receiving care as recommendedin the CPG for MDD
To enhance antidepressant treatment, veterans should be educated on when to take the medication, possible side effects, risks, and the expected duration of treatment, among other things	6 of 30 veterans lacked documentation of patient education when the medication was prescribed
Standardized assessments of depressive symptoms, such as the Patient Health Questionnaire-9, should be used to monitor treatment at 4-6 weeks after initiation of treatment and after each change in treatment	26 of 30 veterans were not assessed using a standardized assessment tool at 4-6 weeks after initiation of treatment 18 of 30 veterans were not assessed using a standardized assessment tool at any encountera 10 of 30 veterans did not have a follow-up encounter that occurred 4-6 weeks after initiation of treatmentb
A plan should be developed that addresses the duration of antidepressant treatment, among other things	1 veteran of 30 did not have a planned date for follow up and plan for future care documented in the veteran's medical record at the initial encounter

Source: GAO analysis of Department of Veterans Affairs (VA) data. | GAO-15-55

Note: We included 30 veterans in our review. Our review began with the encounter during which a VA clinician ordered an antidepressant to treat depressive symptoms (initial encounter) and five follow-up encounters with a VA clinician, or sooner if the veteran did not have five follow-up encounters. Our review was limited to encounters during which the antidepressant treatment was reviewed, including encounters during which side effects and treatment effect were assessed, but no change was made to medication orders.

[a]Of the 30 veterans included in our review, only 6 were assessed using a standardized assessment at the initial encounter where antidepressant medication was prescribed. VA Central Office officials explained that they would expect a standardized assessment to be conducted at the start of an antidepressant to establish a baseline score.

[b]Three veterans did not receive a follow-up appointment at all. Two veterans did not show for scheduled appointments that were within the CPG recommended time frame. Five veterans did not have a follow-up encounter until after 6 weeks.

For example, the CPG recommends that veterans' depressive symptoms be assessed at 4-6 weeks after initiation of antidepressant treatment to determine the efficacy of the treatment. However, medical records of 10 of the 30 veterans we reviewed indicated that they did not have a follow-up encounter within the CPG's recommended 4-6 week time frame. Of those 10 veterans,

- 3 veterans did not have any follow-up encounters related to mental health;
- 2 veterans did not show for scheduled appointments that were within the CPG recommended time frame; and
- 5 veterans did not have a follow-up encounter until after 6 weeks. This follow up ranged from 7 weeks to 50 weeks after the initial encounter.[34]

Some clinicians at VAMCs we visited described instances in which they generally do not follow the CPG recommendations.[35] For example, not all clinicians use a standardized assessment to evaluate a veteran's symptoms. Officials from two VAMCs we visited explained that they do not routinely use the PHQ-9. According to one of these VAMCs, the standard of care is a clinical interview and observation. However, the CPG recommendation states that the PHQ-9 combined with a clinical interview should be used to obtain the necessary information about symptoms and symptom severity. It also states that the PHQ-9 improves diagnostic accuracy and aids treatment decisions by quantifying symptom severity. Furthermore, clinicians may also prefer different time frames for follow up, which are not always consistent with the CPG recommendation. For example, one clinician told us that he tries to see the veteran 3 weeks after the initial appointment, and clinicians at another VAMC like to see the veteran within 6 weeks, but told us that this is sometimes difficult due to scheduling constraints.[36]

VA Lacks Mechanisms to Determine the Extent to Which Veterans Are Receiving Care Consistent with CPG Recommendations

VA does not know the extent to which veterans are receiving care consistent with the MDD CPG. While deviations from recommended practice may be appropriate in many cases due to clinician discretion, VA has not fully assessed whether these examples are acceptable deviations from the CPG. According to the federal internal control standard for risk assessment, agencies should comprehensively identify risks, assess the possible effects, if any, and determine what actions should be taken to mitigate any significant risks. VA Central Office has not developed a mechanism to fully identify deviations that could impede veterans' recovery that may result when VAMCs do not provide care consistent with the MDD CPG. VA Central Office officials explained that the CPG recommendations are guidelines that clinicians can use to inform and guide clinical decision making. VA officials told us that VA cannot require the use of all recommendations in all cases; rather, CPG recommendations should be applied on a case-by-case basis based on the needs of the veteran and with clinician judgment. One official also said it would be difficult to check every CPG recommendation to ensure that clinicians are providing care consistent with the CPG, but stated that VA could identify for review those recommendations that may put veterans' health at risk if not followed.[37] However, with no mechanism to assess whether the care provided is consistent with the CPG, VA is unable to ensure that deviations from recommended care are identified.

While monitoring full compliance with CPG recommendations may be difficult, there are nevertheless ways to address the issue. In fact, VA Central Office and some VAMCs have implemented mechanisms to determine the extent to which veterans are receiving care that is consistent with some of the CPG recommendations; however, these mechanisms do not fully assess all deviations that could impede a veteran's recovery, as illustrated by the following.

- In fiscal year 2014, VA began to review mental health care delivery at VAMCs through a psychopharmacology quality improvement initiative consisting of a series of prescribing practices metrics, although this initiative does not fully assess the extent to which care is consistent with the MDD CPG.[38] One metric—the proportion of veterans with depression prescribed three or more concurrent antidepressant medications for 60 or more continuous days—relates to 2 of the over 200 MDD CPG recommendations.[39] According to one VA Central Office official, the initial phase of the initiative is focused on decreasing variability in prescribing practices among VAMCs. To start the initiative, VA compiled metric profiles for each VAMC, which included a description of how each VAMC performed for all metrics as well as the performance of each VAMC relative to the VISN and national averages. VA requires that all VAMCs address metrics where performance was lower than the national average.

Currently, VA is assisting VAMCs with developing action plans to address these metrics. Because the initiative is in the early stages, it is too soon to determine how VA Central Office and VAMCs will review and remedy deviations from the two CPG recommendations addressed by this initiative. According to VA Central Office officials, the psychopharmacology quality improvement initiative is a mechanism VA currently has to look at CPG recommendations, and VA could add additional metrics addressing other CPG recommendations in the future. However, VA Central Office officials stated that other CPG recommendations would require a more in depth analysis, such as medical record reviews, and it would be difficult to develop metrics for some of the recommendations.[40]

- While VA Central Office does not have a mechanism to determine the extent to which VAMCs are providing care consistent with a majority of the CPG recommendations, some VAMCs have implemented a software system to help ensure that veterans with MDD who are prescribed antidepressants receive care consistent with the CPG when the veteran is treated in a primary care clinic.[41] At the time of our site visits, three of the VAMCs we visited were using such a system—the Behavioral Health Laboratory (BHL).[42] The BHL is designed to manage the behavioral health needs of veterans through telephone or in-person visits. As part of the system, clinicians can use a structured interview—including a PHQ-9—that assesses veterans' mental health symptoms in a way that is consistent with the CPG recommendation for follow-up assessment. Although the BHL can be used to help ensure care is provided consistent with a few of the recommendations in the CPG, the BHL is not used to monitor all veterans prescribed antidepressants. Generally, VAMCs use the BHL to monitor veterans being treated for mental health conditions, such as MDD, in primary care clinics, and to participate, veterans can be referred by their primary care clinician or request to participate.[43]

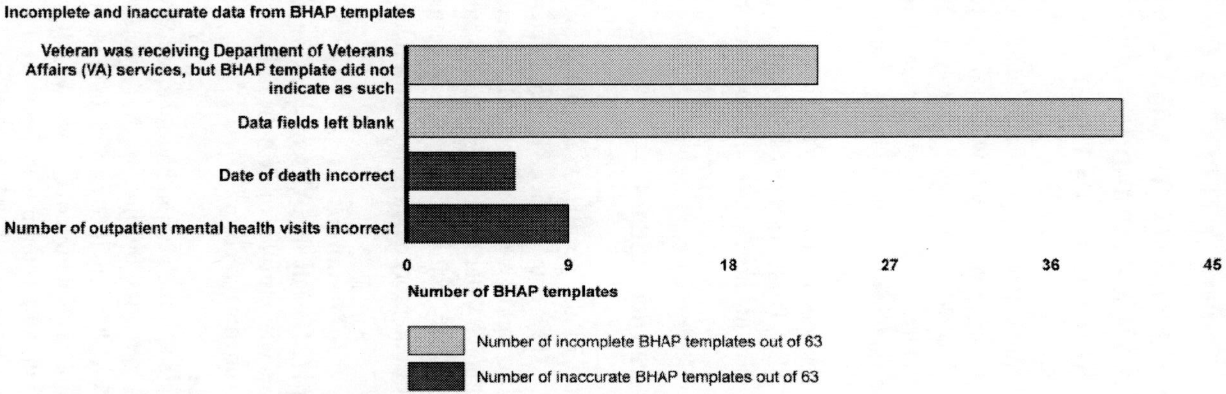

Source: GAO analysis of VA data. | GAO-15-55.

Figure 1. Number of Behavioral Health Autopsy Program (BHAP) Post-Mortem Chart Analysis Templates with Incomplete or Inaccurate Data.

DEMOGRAPHIC AND CLINICAL DATA VA COLLECTS ON VETERAN SUICIDES WERE NOT ALWAYS COMPLETE OR ACCURATE, AND VAMCS APPLIED INSTRUCTIONS FOR GATHERING SUICIDE DATA DIFFERENTLY

We found that demographic, clinical, and other data submitted to VA Central Office on veteran suicides were not always completely or correctly entered into the BHAP Post-Mortem Chart Analysis Templates— a mechanism by which VA Central Office collects veteran suicide data from VAMCs' review of veterans' medical records. (Figure 1 shows the number of BHAP templates we found with incomplete or inaccurate data.) Moreover, VAMCs interpreted and applied instructions for completing the BHAP templates differently. We also found that most VAMCs and VISNs we reviewed and VA Central Office did not review suicide data for accuracy.

Veteran Suicide Data Are Incomplete

We found that over half of the 63 BHAP templates we examined had incomplete information.[44] The data either lacked veteran enrollment information, or other specific fields were omitted. Moreover, the data were lacking entirely for certain known veteran suicides. Incomplete data limits VA Central Office's ability to identify information that can be used to help VA Central Office develop policy and procedures to prevent veteran deaths.

Lack of Veteran Enrollment Information

Approximately one-third (23) of the BHAP templates we reviewed did not indicate whether the veteran was enrolled in VA health care services, even though the veteran had a VA medical record.[45]

- Eight did not indicate that the veteran had received VA services when the templates were submitted by three of the VAMCs in our review, even though these VAMCs provided care to these veterans.
- Fifteen BHAP templates submitted by two VAMCs in our review originally indicated that the veteran was receiving VA care; however, when we reviewed the submitted BHAP templates we received from VA Central Office for the same 15 veterans, the BHAP templates did not indicate that the veteran was being seen in the VA.[46]

VA Central Office used enrollment information when compiling the most recent BHAP interim report, which is part of VA Central Office's quality improvement efforts for its suicide prevention program.[47] Specifically, VA Central Office included clinical data in the BHAP interim report only for veterans utilizing VA services. Therefore, clinical data for the 23 veterans we identified would not be included in the interim report. Missing one-third of the data from its analysis, as was the case in our sample, could have a detrimental effect on the trends VA Central Office reports and uses to improve its suicide prevention efforts.

Requested Data Was Omitted

Forty of the 63 BHAP templates we reviewed included various data fields where no response was provided, resulting in incomplete data. For example, for 19 templates, VAMC staff did not enter requested data as to whether the veteran had all or some of 15 active psychiatric symptoms within 12 months prior to the veteran's date of death. 48 Also, 9 templates did not include an answer for the number of previous suicide attempts by the veteran. Officials from one VAMC told us that they left this field blank if the veteran did not have any previous suicide attempts, rather than entering a "0," even though the BHAP Guide states that officials should enter the appropriate number of previous suicide attempts. Officials at one VAMC told us that fields are sometimes left blank if the standardized answers available on the BHAP template are not adequate; that is, the answer for that veteran does not fit into one of the answers provided on the BHAP template.[49] Officials at two VAMCs stated that it is sometimes easy to overlook fields in the BHAP template, resulting in unanswered questions.

Filling in all fields in the BHAP template, rather than leaving the field blank, is important because some blank fields are counted as "missing" or "no" in the analysis conducted by VA Central Office for the BHAP interim reports. This, in turn, could affect the suicide trends reported. For example, for the number of previous suicide attempts, blank fields are counted as "missing" in the BHAP interim report, rather than "0" previous suicide attempts as officials from one VAMC intended. In other cases, such as for psychiatric symptoms, missing fields are counted as "no," meaning that the veteran did not have these symptoms. In at least one BHAP template, the answer for the psychiatric symptom of isolation was left blank, and would therefore be counted as negative in the interim report despite the fact that officials from the one VAMC told us that the veteran did have this symptom. See figure 2, which provides an excerpt of the fields from the BHAP template in which VAMCs provided incomplete data.

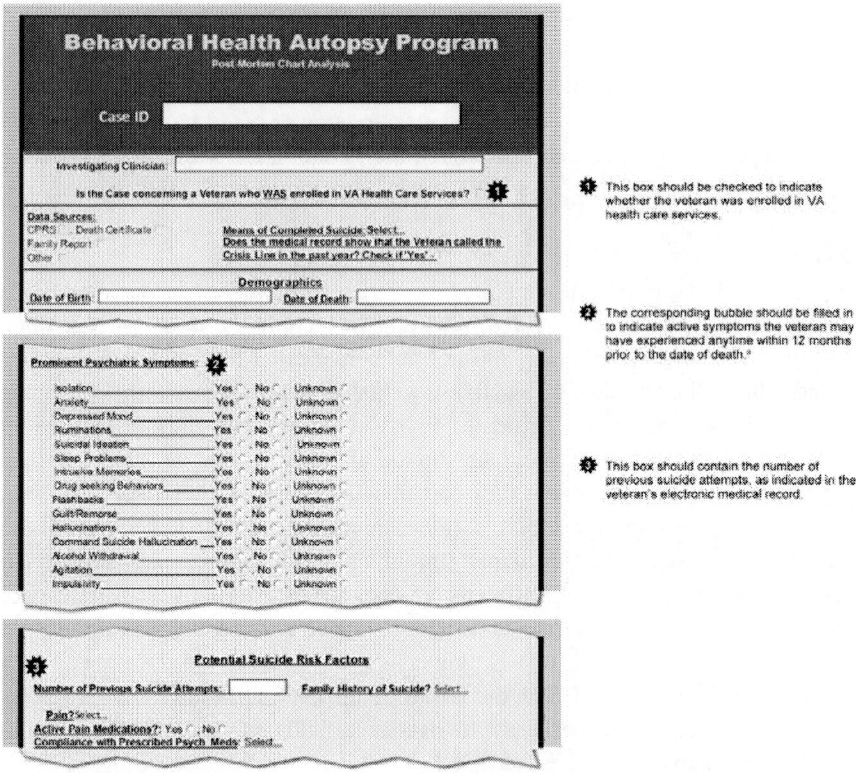

Source: GAO analysis of VA documents. | GAO-15-55.

[a]The BHAP template has changed over time and "unknown" has not always been an option in this section of the BHAP template.

Figure 2. Excerpts of the Department of Veterans Affairs' (VA) Behavioral Health Autopsy Program (BHAP) Template in Which Selected VA Medical Centers Submitted Incomplete Data.

Data Were Lacking Entirely for Certain Known Veteran Suicides

We found that VAMCs did not always submit BHAP templates for all veteran suicides known to the facility, as required by the BHAP Guide. VA Central Office does not have a process in place to determine whether it is receiving the BHAP templates for all known veteran suicides.[50] For example, one VAMC had completed 13 BHAP templates at the time of our site visit but had not submitted them; however, neither the VAMC nor VA Central Office were aware that these templates had not been submitted until after we requested them from VA Central Office. The suicide prevention coordinator at this VAMC told us that the BHAP templates were forwarded to another official at the VAMC, rather than being submitted through VA Central Office's process, and that the BHAP templates were never submitted. As a result of our inquiry, the VAMC submitted these templates to VA Central Office. In another example, officials at a different VAMC told us that, at the time of our site visit, they had recently begun completing and submitting BHAP templates, beginning with veteran suicides occurring in fiscal year 2014. VA Central Office officials told us that VAMCs can start submitting BHAP templates at any point, and officials are not requiring the VAMCs to go back and submit information on all suicides since October 1, 2012. However, this practice is contrary to VA policy, which states that VAMCs should submit BHAP templates for all suicides known to the facility and reported on or after October 1, 2012.

Veteran Suicide Data Are Inaccurate

Of the 63 BHAP templates we reviewed, we found numerous instances of inaccurate data submitted on BHAP templates, as illustrated by the following examples.

- **Incorrect date of death**: Six BHAP templates included a date of death that was incorrect based on information in the veteran's medical record.[51] The difference in the dates of death in the veterans' medical records and the dates of death in the BHAP templates ranged from 1 day to 1 year. For example, one BHAP template indicated that the veteran died in the year after the veteran's actual date of death. Another BHAP template appeared to use the date the suicide behavior report was completed, rather than the veteran's actual date of death. The suicide behavior report was completed 69 days after the veteran's date of death.[52] The accuracy of the date of death recorded in the BHAP template is important because it is used as a point of reference to calculate other fields, such as the number of mental health visits in the last 30 days.
- **Incorrect number of mental health visits**: Nine BHAP templates included the incorrect number of outpatient VA mental health visits in

the last 30 days. [53] For example, one BHAP template indicated that the veteran had five outpatient mental health visits, including three non-mental health visits that should not have been included in the total number of mental health visits for this veteran. Another BHAP template indicated the veteran had been seen once by a mental health provider in the last 30 days; however, we found in reviewing the medical records that this veteran had not been seen by a mental health provider during this time period. This veteran would be included in the BHAP interim report as having a mental health visit, and, as a result, VA's data would include an inaccurate count of the number of veterans with mental health visits in the last 30 days.[54] Without accurate information, VA cannot use this information to determine whether policies or procedures need to be changed to ensure that veterans at high risk for suicide are being seen more frequently by a mental health provider to help prevent suicides in the future.

See figure 3, which provides an excerpt of the fields from the BHAP template in which VAMCs provided inaccurate data.

VAMCs Have Interpreted and Applied Instructions for Completing the BHAP Templates Differently

We found several situations where VAMCs interpreted and applied instructions for completing the BHAP templates differently, as illustrated in the following examples.[55]

- We found inconsistencies in how different VAMCs arrived at answers provided in the BHAP templates. For example, one VAMC included a visit to an immunization clinic as the veteran's final visit, while another VAMC did not include this type of visit, even though this was the last time the veteran was seen in person. The BHAP Guide indicates that the final visit should be the last time the veteran had in-person contact with any VAMC staff, but the BHAP Guide does not identify the different types of visits that should be counted.[56] VA Central Office officials stated that a visit to an immunization clinic should be included as the final visit with the veteran. When VAMCs do not provide consistent data, VA Central Office will receive and use inconsistent data in preparing its trend reports, such as BHAP interim reports, which are intended to be used to improve suicide prevention efforts.

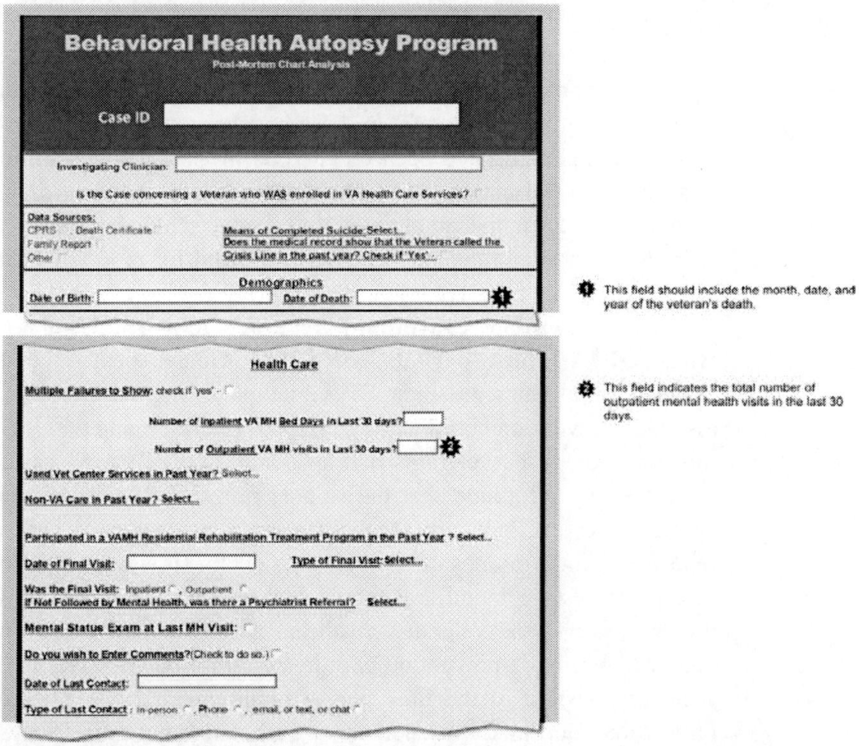
Behavioral Health Autopsy Program
Post-Mortem Chart Analysis
Case ID
Investigating Clinician:
Is the Case concerning a Veteran who WAS enrolled in VA Health Care Services?
Data Sources:
CPRS Death Certificate
Family Report
Other
Means of Completed Suicide: Select...
Does the medical record show that the Veteran called the Crisis Line in the past year? Check if 'Yes' -
Demographics
Date of Birth: Date of Death: 1
Health Care
Multiple Failures to Show: check if 'yes' -
Number of Inpatient VA MH Bed Days in Last 30 days?
Number of Outpatient VA MH visits in Last 30 days? 2
Used Vet Center Services in Past Year? Select...
Non-VA Care in Past Year? Select...
Participated in a VAMH Residential Rehabilitation Treatment Program in the Past Year ? Select...
Date of Final Visit: Type of Final Visit: Select...
Was the Final Visit: Inpatient , Outpatient
If Not Followed by Mental Health, was there a Psychiatrist Referral? Select...
Mental Status Exam at Last MH Visit:
Do you wish to Enter Comments?(Check to do so.)
Date of Last Contact:
Type of Last Contact : in-person , Phone , email, or text, or chat

Source: GAO analysis of VA documents. | GAO-15-55.

Figure 3. Excerpts of the Department of Veterans Affairs' (VA) Behavioral Health Autopsy Program (BHAP) Template in Which Selected VA Medical Centers Submitted Inaccurate Data.

- We also found instances in which BHAP templates included information that did not conform to the instructions in the BHAP Guide on how to complete the BHAP medical record reviews.
  - **Last contact did not always represent the last time a VAMC official spoke with the veteran**: The BHAP Guide instructions specify that the last contact recorded in the BHAP template should be the last recorded interaction with the veteran, which could be in person, through a phone call, or through email. Five of the 63 BHAP templates we reviewed did not indicate the last

time an official spoke directly to the veteran. One BHAP template counted a phone call with a veteran's spouse after the veteran's death as the last contact with the veteran. The BHAP template also counted this phone conversation as an "in-person" interaction. The remaining four BHAP templates included a date for the last contact that was prior to the date for the veteran's final in-person visit at the VAMC. In these instances, the veterans' in-person visit should have been counted as the last contact. From this flawed information, VA would not be able to determine reliable trends for the amount of time between the last contact with the veteran and the veteran's date of death for reports that it prepares, such as the BHAP interim report.

- **Suicide prevention coordinator contact and referral not within BHAP time period**: The BHAP Guide specifies that VAMCs should indicate in the BHAP template whether there was a suicide prevention coordinator contact or referral made within 3 months prior to the veteran's date of death. In 3 of the 63 cases we reviewed, we found that the suicide prevention coordinators checked the box indicating that they saw the veteran or had a referral within 3 months of the veteran's death. However, in each of these cases we found that the contact was made more than 3 months prior to the veteran's death, so it should not have been counted. A suicide prevention coordinator from one VAMC said she was unaware of the time period requirement and a suicide prevention coordinator at another VAMC stated that time frames should be added to the BHAP template, rather than just included in the BHAP Guide. The BHAP interim reports include the number of veterans that had a suicide prevention coordinator contact or referral, and by including information on contacts or referrals that are outside the BHAP Guide time frame, these reports may be at risk of misreporting trends in this area.

See figure 4, which provides an excerpt of the fields from the BHAP template in which VAMCs provided inconsistent data.

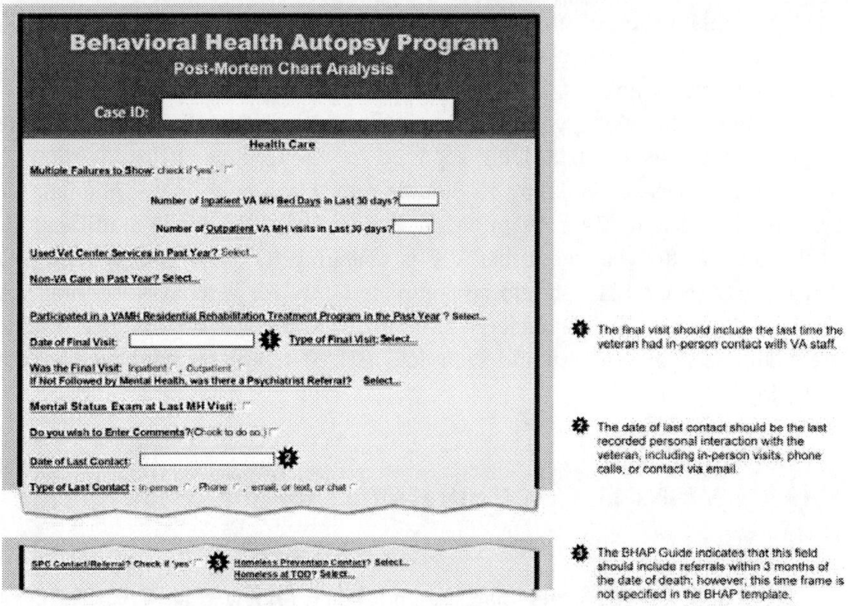

Source: GAO analysis of VA documents. | GAO-15-55.

Figure 4. Excerpts of the Department of Veterans Affairs' (VA) Behavioral Health Autopsy Program (BHAP) Template in Which Selected VA Medical Centers Submitted Inconsistent Data.

VA policy and guidance states that the BHAP template should be completed for all suicides known to the facility, but at the five VAMCs we visited, these data were not always being reported.[57] However, the policy and instructions do not explicitly state that veterans not being seen by VA should be included, and in the absence of this declaration, some VAMCs interpreted the instructions to mean that only veterans being seen by VA should be included in the data submitted. Therefore, two VAMCs have submitted data only for veterans being treated by VA, while the others include data on all known veteran suicides—whether they have been treated by VA or not. This further adds to the inconsistencies in the information that VAMCs submit on the BHAP templates. VA Central Office officials told us that BHAP templates should be completed for both veterans utilizing VA health care services, as well as those veterans not being seen in the VA, and that this requirement has been discussed at training sessions and during conference calls with suicide prevention coordinators. For example, during a suicide prevention conference in November 2013, a VA Central Office official informed participants that the

BHAP template should be completed for all suicides reported through SPAN, which VA Central Office officials previously told us includes veterans that were not receiving VA care. The inconsistency in VAMC officials' understanding of which veterans should have a completed BHAP template results in inconsistent data being reported to VA Central Office. While VA was in the process of updating its suicide prevention coordinator manual, we brought this issue to VA's attention. In August 2014, VA made modifications to the manual that indicated that VA is changing its policy—now requiring that the BHAP template should be completed only for veterans receiving VA services. However, the guidance continues to be unclear on whether suicide prevention coordinators should complete BHAP templates for veterans not receiving VA care.[58]

VAMCs, VISNs, and VA Central Office Do Not Review Suicide Data

We found that BHAP templates are not being reviewed by VA officials at any level for accuracy, completeness, and consistency. Therefore, our findings at five VAMCs could be symptomatic nationwide and other VAMCs may also be submitting incomplete, inaccurate, and inconsistent suicide-related information and VA may not be getting the data it needs across the Department to make appropriate resource decisions and develop new policy. VA policy states that it is the VISN's and VAMC's decision whether to conduct reviews of BHAP data prior to submission to VA Central Office. With few exceptions, VAMCs and VISNs we visited generally do not conduct data checks on the information submitted in the BHAP templates. Additionally, VA Central Office does not review the information for accuracy and completeness in the BHAP templates it receives. This approach is inconsistent with internal control standards for the federal government, which state that agencies should have controls over information processes, including procedures and standards to ensure the completeness and accuracy of processed data.[59]

Officials at one VAMC told us that VAMC staff compare the BHAP data and the veteran's medical record prior to submitting the BHAP template to VA Central Office to ensure accuracy. In response to our review, another VAMC implemented a procedure to check the accuracy and completeness of their BHAP templates prior to submission. The procedure at this VAMC requires the suicide prevention coordinator and case manager to independently complete the BHAP template and compare their responses. The BHAP templates are then reviewed by the Assistant Mental Health Clinic Director prior to submission.

We also found that VA lacks sufficient controls to ensure the quality of the existing BHAP data. For example, VA Central Office officials said there are no automated data checks to ensure the accuracy of data it uses for the BHAP interim report, such as checking to ensure that the date of last contact with the veteran that is recorded in the BHAP template is not after the veteran's date of death. Although officials removed apparent duplicates in submitted BHAP templates by matching the veteran's name and social security number while compiling the data for the most recent BHAP interim report, they do not conduct data checks to help identify some of the incomplete or inaccurate data we found in our review.

CONCLUSION

Given the negative effects of MDD, it is important to provide timely, evidence-based treatment for veterans with MDD, and VA's ability to monitor these veterans is critical to ensuring positive outcomes. However, our findings demonstrate that VA may not be fully aware of the population of veterans with MDD due to a lack of coding precision by clinicians. This can limit VA's ability to assess the Department's performance in treating veterans as recommended in the MDD CPG and in measuring health outcomes for veterans. Additionally, VA does not have mechanisms in place to ensure that the Department is able to identify deviations from CPG-recommended care and remedy those that could impede veterans' recovery. Even if VA did have mechanisms in place, the coding discrepancies we identified would limit VA's ability to extract accurate data on all veterans diagnosed with MDD, therefore hindering VA's ability to determine the extent to which veterans are receiving care consistent with the CPG recommendations for MDD. The CPG recommendations are meant to improve veteran outcomes by providing maximum relief from the debilitating symptoms of MDD, and VA cannot ensure that the care veterans receive is consistent with those recommendations.

The existence of incomplete, inaccurate, and inconsistent information submitted through VA's BHAP templates limits the Department's ability to accurately evaluate its suicide prevention efforts and identify trends in veteran suicides through the BHAP initiative. Specifically, data drawn from incomplete, inaccurate, and inconsistent BHAP templates limit the Department's opportunities to learn from past veteran suicides and ultimately diminish efforts to improve its suicide prevention activities. VAMCs, VISNs, and VA Central Office generally lack a process to ensure that the data that are submitted and used by VA Central Office to identify trends in veteran suicides are complete, accurate, and consistent. Checking and verifying the data submitted to VA Central Office would help ensure that changes made to suicide prevention efforts by VAMCs, VISNs, and VA are based on actual trends in veteran suicides. Without clear VA Central Office instructions to guide how VAMCs and VISNs should complete BHAP templates and report suicide data, the validity of suicide data and the effectiveness of VA's actions will be hampered.

RECOMMENDATIONS FOR EXECUTIVE ACTION

We recommend that the Secretary of Veterans Affairs direct the Under Secretary for Health to take the following six actions:

To more accurately estimate the prevalence of MDD and identify enrolled veterans with MDD, VA should

- identify the extent to which there is imprecise diagnostic coding of MDD by further examining encounters with a diagnostic code of depression not otherwise specified, which could be incorporated into VAMCs' ongoing review of diagnostic coding accuracy, and
- determine and address the factor(s) contributing to the imprecise coding based on the results of those examinations. For example, feedback and additional training could be provided to clinicians regarding the importance of diagnostic code accuracy, or VA's medical record could be enhanced to facilitate the selection of a more accurate diagnostic code.

To ensure that veterans are receiving care in accordance with the MDD CPG, VA should

- implement processes to review data on veterans with MDD prescribed antidepressants to evaluate the level of risk of any deviations from recommended care and remedy those that could impede veterans' recovery.

To improve VA's efforts to inform its suicide prevention activities, VA should

- ensure that VAMCs have a process in place to review data on veteran suicides for completeness, accuracy, and consistency before the data are submitted to VA Central Office,
- clarify guidance on how to complete BHAP templates to ensure that VAMCs are submitting consistent data on veteran suicides, and
- implement processes to review data on veteran suicides submitted by VAMCs for accuracy and completeness.

AGENCY COMMENTS

We provided a draft of this report to VA for comment. In its written comments, VA generally agreed with our conclusions and concurred with our recommendations. In addition, VA provided information on its plans for implementing each recommendation, with estimated completion dates in calendar year 2015.

Sincerely yours,
Randall B. Williamson
Director, Health Care

APPENDIX I: SCOPE AND METHODOLOGY

Characteristics of Veterans Diagnosed with Major Depressive Disorder (MDD)

To describe the characteristics of veterans diagnosed with MDD from fiscal years 2009 through 2013, we analyzed Department of Veterans Affairs (VA) and Department of Defense (DOD) data. (See table 3.) These data included information on veterans' demographic characteristics as well as clinical information on health care services and medications provided through VA.[1] Veterans were classified as having a diagnosis of MDD if, in at least one fiscal year included in our review, they had two or more outpatient encounters or at least one inpatient hospital stay with a diagnosis of MDD.[2]

Table 3. Description of Department of Veterans Affairs and Department of Defense Data Files Used to Examine Characteristics of Veterans with Major Depressive Disorder for Fiscal Years 2009 through 2013

Data files	Description
Demographic files	Includes information extracted from the Department of Veterans Affairs (VA) Corporate Data Warehouse on veterans' age; date of death, if applicable; sex; race; and ethnicity. The Corporate Data Warehouse is a national data repository comprising data from several VA clinical and administrative systems. Information on whether veterans served during recent conflicts in Iraq and Afghanistan was obtained from a Department of Defense roster.
Medical SAS Inpatient Datasets, Acute Care Dataset	Includes information on acute care inpatient stays at VA medical centers (VAMC) that lastat least 24 hours, including admission and discharge date as well as diagnosis codes. This dataset comprises information on inpatient care that is entered into veterans' electronic medical records by staff at VAMCs.
Fee basis inpatient filesa	Includes information on certain acute care inpatient stays at non-VAMCs, including admission and discharge dates as well as diagnostic codes. VA pays for these stays at non-VAMCs when VA cannot offer needed care, when a non-VA provider would be economical, or on an emergency basis when travel to a VA facility is medically infeasible. The fee basis inpatient files for each fiscal year are limited to information on inpatient stays at non-VAMCs that were paid for by VA during the corresponding fiscal year.
Outpatient encounter files	Includes information on outpatient services rendered by VA providers, including the date of the services and diagnoses treated. This file comprises information on individual outpatient encounters entered into veterans' electronic medical records by staff at VA medical facilities. Encounters are defined as a professional contact between a patient and a VA provider with responsibility for diagnosing, evaluating, and treating veterans' conditions.
Fee basis outpatient services filesa	Includes information on certain outpatient care rendered by non-VA providers, including the date of the visit and the reason for the visit. VA pays for these services from non-VA providers when VA cannot offer needed care, when a non-VA provider would be economical, or on an emergency basis when travel to a VA facility is medically infeasible. The fee basis outpatient services files for each fiscal year are limited to information on outpatient encounters that were paid for by VA during the corresponding fiscal year.

Data files	Description
Pharmacy Benefits Management prescription database	Includes information on medications ordered by VA providers, including medication name and dosage instructions. The pharmacy database comprises information on medication orders, which are entered into local pharmacy databases by staff at VA medical facilities.

Source: GAO. | GAO-15-55

[a]The two data sets have retained the name fee basis though VA now refers to this type of care as non-VA medical care.

Specifically, we examined the following:

- **Number of veterans diagnosed with MDD**. We used a demographic file provided by VA to determine the number of veterans diagnosed with MDD.
- **Characteristics of veterans diagnosed with MDD**. We used demographic files provided by VA and DOD to describe characteristics of veterans diagnosed with MDD. In particular, the veteran characteristics we examined included the following:
  - **Age**. We created seven categories for veterans' ages as of September 30, 2013—the end of fiscal year 2013, which corresponds to the last date of data we included in our analysis. These categories are as follows: (a) 18-24, (b) 25-34, (c) 35-44, (d) 45-54, (e) 55-64, (f) 65-74, and (g) 75 and older.
  - **Era of service**. We categorized veterans as either being veterans of the recent conflicts in Iraq and Afghanistan—Operation Iraqi Freedom, Operation Enduring Freedom, and Operation New Dawn—or of other eras of service.[3]
  - **Sex**. We categorized veterans as either being female or male.
  - **Race and ethnicity**. We created categories to describe veterans' race and ethnicity (Hispanic and non-Hispanic). These categories are consistent with the Office of Management and Budget's 1997 *Standards for Maintaining, Collecting, and Presenting Federal Data on Race and Ethnicity*.[4]
- **Extent to which veterans diagnosed with MDD were prescribed at least one antidepressant**. Using data from the Pharmacy Benefits Management database, we examined the extent to which VA providers prescribed at least one antidepressant for veterans diagnosed with MDD from fiscal years 2009 through 2013. This includes

antidepressants prescribed to treat depression as well as those prescribed to treat other conditions.[5]

- **The percentage of veterans with MDD dispensed a 12-week and a 6-month supply of an antidepressant**. Using VA data we obtained from the Medical SAS Inpatient Datasets, Acute Care Dataset; Outpatient Encounter Files; Fee Basis Outpatient and Inpatient Services Files; and Pharmacy Benefits Management Database, we calculated the percentage of veterans with MDD dispensed a 12-week and a 6-month supply of an antidepressant according to statistical programming logic provided by VA.[6] These measures are intended to assess the effectiveness of antidepressant medication management and are based on performance measures developed by the National Committee for Quality Assurance.[7] In addition, these measures are consistent with the *VA/DOD Clinical Practice Guideline for Management of Major Depressive Disorder*, which indicates that continued antidepressant treatment, after acute depressive symptoms have resolved, decreases the incidence of relapse of MDD.[8]

We selected six VA medical centers (VAMC) at the following locations to visit: Canandaigua, New York; Gainesville, Florida; Iowa City, Iowa; Philadelphia, Pennsylvania; Phoenix, Arizona; and Reno, Nevada.[9] These VAMCs represent different facility complexity groups, serve populations of veterans that differ in terms of the extent of use of mental health services, and are located in different Veterans Integrated Service Networks (VISN), or regional networks of care.[10] To gather additional perspectives, for each VAMC we visited, we selected one associated community-based outpatient clinic to visit. In particular, we visited community-based outpatient clinics in the following locations: Cedar Rapids, Iowa; Globe, Arizona; Gloucester, New Jersey; Lecanto, Florida; Fallon, Nevada; and Rochester, New York. (See table 4.) As part of our site visits, we reviewed a nongeneralizeable sample of five medical records for each of these six VAMCs for a total of 30 veterans.[11] We reviewed these medical records to determine if the diagnostic code entered for all encounters— starting with the initial encounter in 2012 when the veteran was diagnosed with MDD and prescribed an antidepressant—was consistent with a diagnosis of MDD.

Table 4. Characteristics of Veterans Affairs Medical Centers (VAMC) and Community-Based Outpatient Clinics Selected for GAO's Review

VAMC location	Facility complexity group, 2011	Percentage of veterans that used mental health services, 2012 (above or below average)	Veterans Integrated Service Network (VISN)	Community-based outpatient clinic location
Canandaigua, New York	3	24.6 (above)	2	Rochester, New York
Gainesville, Florida[a]	1a	22.2 (below)	8	Lecanto, Florida[a]
Iowa City, Iowa	1c	16.7 (below)	23	Cedar Rapids, Iowa
Philadelphia, Pennsylvania	1b	28.3 (above)	4	Gloucester, New Jersey
Phoenix, Arizona	1c	24.3 (above)	18	Globe, Arizona
Reno, Nevada[a]	2	22.4 (below)	21	Fallon, Nevada[a]

Source: GAO analysis of VA data. | GAO-15-55

Note: The Department of Veterans Affairs (VA) assigns each VAMC a complexity score between 1 and 3, with level 1 being the most complex, using a facility complexity model. Level 1 is broken down further into 1a, 1b, and 1c. That model uses multiple variables to measure facility complexity arrayed along four categories, namely patient population served, clinical services offered, education and research complexity, and administrative complexity. Each VAMC is assigned to a single regional network of care, called a VISN.

[a]In contrast to the other site visits, which were conducted in person, we conducted a virtual site visit via telephone interviews to these locations.

To select medical records for review, we completed the following steps:

- Randomly generated a list of individuals with a new prescription for an antidepressant in calendar year 2012.
- Selected the first five individuals in the list that met the following inclusion criteria:
    - Veteran status.
    - Had a diagnosis of MDD in calendar year 2012. For the purposes of medical record reviews, we classified a veteran as having a diagnosis of MDD if, based on how the veteran's patient care encounters were coded or on the narrative contained in clinical notes in the veteran's medical record, the veteran had (a) at least

two outpatient encounters with a diagnosis of MDD, or (b) at least one inpatient stay with a diagnosis of MDD.[12]

- Had a new treatment episode of antidepressants in calendar year 2012. New treatment episodes were defined as an initiation of antidepressant treatment following a period during which the veteran was either (1) not prescribed an antidepressant or (2) noncompliant with and had not picked up prescriptions for a previously prescribed antidepressant.

To ensure the reliability of the data we analyzed, we interviewed VA Central Office officials, reviewed relevant documentation and veterans' medical records, and conducted electronic testing to identify missing data and obvious errors. On the basis of these activities, we determined that the data we analyzed were sufficiently reliable for our purposes. However, as discussed in the report, we described limitations of the data due to the coding discrepancies we found.

VA's Oversight of the Extent to Which Veterans with MDD Prescribed Antidepressants Are Receiving Care As Recommended in the CPG

To examine the extent to which VAMCs are providing care to veterans with MDD who are prescribed antidepressants as recommended in the CPG, we reviewed relevant VA policy documents. On the basis of that review, we found that VA policy requires all care sites, VAMCs, and community-based outpatient clinics to provide evidence-based antidepressant treatment when indicated for depression and that such care must be consistent with current VA clinical practice guidelines.[13] The relevant VA clinical practice guideline, the *VA/DOD Clinical Practice Guideline for Management of Major Depressive Disorder*, provides evidence-based recommendations for providers on how to monitor veterans prescribed antidepressants; these recommendations are based on a review of depression research outcomes. These recommendations are based on available research at the time of publication of the guideline and are intended to provide information to assist providers in treatment decision-making.[14] From the guideline's recommendations related to monitoring veterans prescribed antidepressants, we judgmentally selected three recommendations for inclusion in our review. In particular, we selected recommendations that (1) had among the highest strength of research evidence, (2) were sufficiently specific to enable us to determine the extent to which VA providers were following the recommendation, and (3) would not require clinical judgment to determine the extent to which VA providers were following the recommendation. The following recommendations were included in our review:

- To enhance antidepressant treatment, veterans should be educated on when to take the medication, possible side effects, risks, and the expected duration of treatment, among other things;
- Standardized assessments of depressive symptoms, such as the Patient Health Questionnaire-9, should be used to monitor treatment response at 4-6 weeks after initiation of treatment, after each change in treatment, and periodically thereafter until full remission is achieved; and
- A plan should be developed that addresses the duration of antidepressant treatment, among other things.

After selecting these recommendations for our review, we examined the extent to which veterans were receiving care consistent with these CPG recommendations at the six VAMCs we visited.[15] To do this, we interviewed VAMC clinicians to determine whether and how they were following these recommendations. At each VAMC, officials interviewed included members of the executive leadership team, primary care and mental health providers, and pharmacists.[16]

Additionally, as part of our examination of the extent to which VAMCs are providing care consistent with the selected guideline recommendations, we reviewed the sample of five veterans' medical records per VAMC used as part of our review of MDD coding. For each medical record, we reviewed documentation contained in the selected veterans' medical records to assess the extent to which the antidepressant treatment-related care VA providers rendered was consistent with the selected CPG recommendations included in our review. Our review commenced with the encounter during which a VA clinician ordered an antidepressant to treat depressive symptoms. Our review ended after five follow-up encounters with a VA clinician, or sooner if the veteran did not have five follow-up encounters. Our review was limited to encounters during which the antidepressant treatment was reviewed, including encounters during which side effects and treatment effect were assessed, but no change was made to medication orders. We did not include, for example, an encounter with an orthopedist during which the fact that the veteran had been prescribed an antidepressant was simply noted. We provided the VAMCs with the instances where we found the medical record documentation was not consistent with the selected CPG recommendations. The VAMCs confirmed our answers or provided additional support if they believed the care was consistent with the CPG.

To examine VA's oversight of the care VAMCs provide to veterans with MDD who are prescribed an antidepressant, we reviewed VA's oversight of the *Uniform Mental Health Services in VA Medical Centers and Clinics* handbook and CPG requirements and evaluated whether this oversight provides VA with adequate information to identify nonconformance with recommended practices, assess the risk of any nonconformance, and address nonconformance, as appropriate.[17] As part of this review, we reviewed VA's oversight in the context of federal standards for internal control for risk assessment.[18] The internal control for risk assessment refers to an agency's ability to comprehensively identify risks, assess the possible effect, if any, and determine what actions should be taken to mitigate significant risks.

We then interviewed officials from VA Central Office, including officials from the Office of Mental Health Services (OMHS), the Office of Mental Health Operations, and the Office of Analytics and Business Intelligence; and the six VISNs that oversee the VAMCs we visited who are responsible for overseeing compliance with VA's requirements, including VA's requirement that all VA facilities provide evidence-based antidepressant treatment when indicated for depression and that such care be consistent with current VA clinical practice guidelines. Through our interviews, we obtained information on the oversight activities conducted by VA Central Office and the extent to which VA Central Office followed up with VAMCs to ensure that they corrected problems identified through these oversight activities. In addition, we obtained and reviewed relevant documents regarding VA oversight, including internal reports and VAMCs' plans to correct problems identified through oversight activities.

INFORMATION VA REQUIRES VAMCS TO COLLECT ON VETERAN SUICIDES

To analyze the information VA requires VAMCs to collect on veteran suicides, we first reviewed VA policies, guidance, and documents related to

VA's suicide prevention efforts to identify the mechanisms by which VA collects veteran suicide data from VAMCs. We also interviewed VA Central Office and other officials responsible for VA's suicide prevention program, including officials from OMHS and the Center of Excellence for Suicide Prevention. We also interviewed VAMC officials and relevant staff of the six VISNs for the sites we visited to obtain information on suicide prevention initiatives.

Next, through the site visits to six VAMCs, we obtained documents and interviewed officials regarding the collection of veteran suicide data. We obtained all completed templates from the Behavioral Health Autopsy Program (BHAP) related to VA's collection of data on veterans that died by suicide as of the time of our site visit or at the time we requested the documents for virtual site visits.[19] One VAMC had not completed any of these BHAP documents because they had not had a veteran die by suicide since the beginning of the program. Therefore, our analysis includes a review of documents from five of the six VAMCs we visited. Through review of the documents, we noted any fields missing data, such as a field that requires a yes or no answer but neither answer is provided.

Additionally, using professional judgment, we identified fields in the documents to review based on whether the field related to aspects of VA treatment—including treatment for mental health conditions—and the date of the veteran's death.[20] We identified these fields because they did not require clinical judgment to assess. Using the parameters in the corresponding guide for filling out these documents, including time frames, we compared these fields to information included in the veteran's medical record and noted differences between our answers and the answers provided by the VAMCs in the documents.

To ensure that we received the final, submitted versions, we also requested these documents from VA Central Office for each of the five VAMCs. We compared these documents to the documents we received from the VAMCs. We used the documents from the VAMCs as the starting point; therefore, we only analyzed the templates for veterans identified by the VAMCs. 21 During the course of our review we learned that the template for these documents had changed over time. If additional fields were included in the templates obtained from VA Central Office, but were not originally included in the templates obtained from the VAMCs, we did not review these fields. We generally used the answer from the document obtained from VA Central Office, which is the final submitted version, unless a field originally had an answer in the template from the VAMC, but was blank or not answered in the template from VA Central Office. In those cases, we used the answer from the VAMC document.

We provided the VAMCs with the fields where the answers in the VAMC's documents did not match our answers based on our review of the medical record. The VAMCs confirmed our answers or provided additional support for their original answer. Results from our review of veteran suicide data can be generalized to the VAMCs we visited, but cannot be generalized to other VAMCs.

We conducted this performance audit from November 2013 to November 2014 in accordance with generally accepted government auditing standards. Those standards require that we plan and perform the audit to obtain sufficient, appropriate evidence to provide a reasonable basis for our findings and conclusions based on our audit objectives. We believe that the evidence obtained provides a reasonable basis for our findings and conclusions based on our audit objectives.

APPENDIX II: DEPARTMENT OF VETERANS AFFAIRS MEDICAL CENTERS' TRACKING OF VETERANS AT HIGH RISK FOR SUICIDE

The Department of Veterans Affairs' (VA) *Uniform Mental Health Services in VA Medical Centers and Clinics* handbook (Handbook) requires VA medical centers (VAMC) to have a suicide prevention coordinator whose responsibilities include establishing and maintaining a list of veterans assessed to be at high risk for suicide and monitoring these veterans.[1] The Handbook also requires suicide prevention coordinators to ensure that providers follow up on missed appointments for high-risk veterans to ensure patient safety and in order to initiate problem-solving about any tensions or difficulties in the veteran's ongoing care.

Whether a veteran is determined to be at high risk for suicide is based on clinical judgment made after an evaluation of risk factors—such as history of past suicide attempts or recent discharge from an inpatient mental health unit—protective factors—such as positive social support, positive coping skills, and positive therapeutic relationships—and the presence or absence of warning signs. Indicators that a veteran is at high risk for suicide include a current verified report or witnessed suicide attempt; identification of current serious suicidal ideation that requires an immediate change in the treatment plan, such as hospitalization; and the presence of any of the following warning signs: threatening to hurt or plan to kill oneself; looking for specific ways to kill oneself and seeking access to such means, such as pills or weapons; and talking or writing about death, dying, or suicide when these actions are out of the ordinary for the person.

The Handbook requires each VAMC to have a process for establishing a patient record flag to help ensure that veterans determined to be at high risk for suicide are provided with follow up for all missed mental health and substance abuse appointments. The primary purpose of the patient record flag is to communicate to staff that a veteran is at high risk for suicide and VA policy states that the presence of a flag should be considered when making treatment decisions. Suicide prevention coordinators are responsible for assessing, in conjunction with the treating clinician, the risk of suicide in individual veterans, ensuring these veterans have a "High Risk for Suicide" Patient Record Flag on their medical record, and reviewing the list of high-risk veterans at least every 90 days.

We interviewed suicide prevention coordinators as part of our site visits with six VAMCs to obtain information on how they track veterans determined to be at high risk for suicide. At four of the VAMCs we visited, suicide prevention coordinators used an electronic spreadsheet to track information on these veterans. For example, the spreadsheets include information such as whether the veteran has a patient record flag on their medical record and when the flag needs to be reviewed, the date for the veteran's next scheduled follow-up appointment, whether the veteran has a safety plan, and the veteran's assigned psychiatrist.[2] Officials from one VAMC told us that they maintain the list daily, adding and removing veterans as necessary. Officials stated that the circumstances under which a veteran would be removed from the spreadsheet varied, but veterans are generally removed because their patient record flag has been removed and the officials no longer consider the veteran to be at high risk for suicide.

The two remaining VAMCs use other mechanisms to track veterans at high risk for suicide. Officials from one VAMC told us that they use the Suicide Prevention Application Network (SPAN) to query high-risk patients at the VAMC. The SPAN database contains veteran information, demographic characteristics, and information on suicide attempts and completed suicides, among other things. According to officials, the information for each veteran in SPAN includes the date the veteran was assessed as being at high risk, as well as the date that the veteran needs to be seen for follow up, if applicable. After our site visit, officials told us they plan to periodically pull a list of all veterans with an active high risk flag in VA's medical record for the VAMC and cross-reference that list to veterans being tracked for high suicide risk by the suicide prevention coordinator in SPAN to ensure all high-risk veterans are tracked. Officials from the other VAMC told us that their case managers each have their own list of veterans that they track and the suicide prevention coordinator we spoke with stated that he does not keep a master list of all veterans that are at high risk for suicide. 3

Appendix III: Department of Veterans Affairs' Use of Data Related to Suicides and Suicide Behavior

Veterans Affairs medical centers (VAMC) collect and submit data on veteran suicides to the Department of Veterans Affairs (VA) Central Office through the Suicide Prevention Application Network (SPAN) and suicide behavior reports.[1] VAMCs also collect and report data through root cause analyses.[2] Additionally, VA Central Office uses the data from SPAN to prepare reports that are sent to the VAMCs and Veterans Integrated Service Networks (VISN).[3] VA Central Office officials stated that they expect VAMCs and VISNs to use these reports and collected data to improve suicide prevention efforts and program evaluation. Through site visits at six VAMCs that we conducted as part of our review and through interviews with corresponding VISN officials, we identified examples of how some VAMCs and VISNs are utilizing veteran suicide data to improve their suicide prevention efforts.

- VAMC and VISN officials have used SPAN to create initiatives based on trends in the data. For example,
  - Officials at one VAMC stated that they use the information collected in SPAN to provide data for performing statistical analyses on the outreach conducted, to study suicide attempts and completions across the VAMC catchment area, to understand the means by which veterans are dying by suicide, and to study the use of high-risk flags.
  - Officials at a VISN explained that through a review of the SPAN data about a year ago, officials learned that 60 percent of suicides in the VISN were completed using a gun. After conducting research on the subject, the VISN began a firearm safety

initiative, which includes notifying veterans by mail that they can receive four gun locks each upon request, with no questions asked.

- VAMC officials have made programmatic changes to their suicide prevention efforts based on trends in the suicide data they are collecting and reviewing. For example,
  - At one VAMC, officials told us that they reviewed suicide behavior reports and, as a result of trends identified in these reports, drafted a policy for medication restriction for veterans at risk of overdosing. Specifically, over a 3-year period, five or six veterans receiving VA care repeatedly attempted suicide by overdose, typically when they were intoxicated. VAMC officials created a work group to draft policy that mitigates risk for medication overdose among high-risk veterans. At the time of our site visit, the group was exploring creating a patient record flag that would be included in the veteran's medical record for overdose risk indicating that medication supplies should be restricted for these veterans and the possibility of using automated pill dispensers to dispense medications to these veterans.
  - Through their work reviewing suicide-related information, the suicide prevention team at another VAMC identified a trend in its suicide data. In particular, they noted that some veterans were given a 90-day supply of the same medications that the veteran recently tried to use to overdose. The suicide prevention team mentioned this to a clinical pharmacist who had also noticed this issue. The VAMC is now trying to restrict days of supply for these types of veterans, but there is no formal policy about this and no plans to craft such a policy. Additionally, officials from this VAMC stated that they have added items to the standardized suicide behavior report template to help them to collect additional useful information, such as active medications and pain score at the time of the last visit.
  - Officials from one VAMC stated that through a review of medical records and autopsy reports for veterans who died by suicide, they found that a vast majority of veterans who died by suicide were not being seen by a mental health provider. In response, officials provided education to primary care providers. VAMC officials also noticed that veterans receiving care for pain were dying by suicide at a high rate. As a result, the VAMC has started an

initiative with the pain clinic, and, as part of this initiative, the chief of the pain management clinic consults with psychiatry on veterans at risk for suicide.

- Officials at a VISN described changes made in response to the suicide data in fiscal year 2012, which showed that a percentage of veterans who completed suicide had no ongoing mental health care.

These veterans mainly received care from VA primary care providers. To address this, the VISN partnered with the Center of Excellence for Suicide Prevention and local university psychologists to help VA primary care providers at community-based outpatient clinics formulate mental health plans.

End Notes

[1] For purposes of this report, references to VAMCs include the associated community-based outpatient clinics.

[2] VA/Department of Defense (DOD) Assessment and Management of Risk for Suicide Working Group, *VA/DOD Clinical Practice Guideline for Assessment and Management of Patients at Risk for Suicide* (June 2013).

[3] Data on whether veterans served during recent conflicts in Iraq and Afghanistan came from DOD.

[4] The data include health care services and medications provided by non-VA providers but paid for by VA through its Non-VA Medical Care Program, formerly known as the Fee Basis Program. Non-VA medical care is the practice of paying for veterans' health care services outside of VA when VA medical facilities are not feasibly available.

[5] The definition of MDD as defined in the fourth edition of the *Diagnostic and Statistical Manual of Mental Disorders* was effective for a majority of the time period that our study covers. According to the American Psychiatric Association, the core symptoms and duration of these symptoms to meet the definition of MDD have not changed from the fourth to fifth edition of the manual. American Psychiatric Association, *Diagnostic and Statistical Manual of Mental Disorders*, 4th ed., Text Revision (DSM-IV-TR) (Washington, D.C.: American Psychiatric Association, 2000).

[6] Throughout the report, we use the phrase medical records to refer to electronic medical records.

[7] In contrast to the other site visits, which were completed in person, we completed the site visits to the VAMCs located in Gainesville, Florida, and Reno, Nevada, virtually through telephone interviews.

[8] The MDD CPG is formally known as the *VA/DOD Clinical Practice Guideline for Management of Major Depressive Disorder* (May, 2009). The MDD CPG was issued by the joint VA/DOD Evidence-Based Practice Work Group in 2009. Formed in 1999 and composed of VA and DOD officials, the VA/DOD Evidence-Based Practice Work Group makes decisions about which CPGs for specific conditions will be developed and oversees their development. VA's Office of Mental Health Services is responsible for developing mental

health policy and the Office of Mental Health Operations (OMHO) is responsible for implementing these policies.

[9] The three recommendations related to monitoring veterans prescribed antidepressants from the CPG that we judgmentally selected were (1) to enhance antidepressant treatment, veterans should be educated on when to take the medication, possible side effects, risks, and the expected duration of treatment; (2) standardized assessments of depressive symptoms should be used to monitor treatment response at 4-6 weeks after initiation of treatment, after each change in treatment, and periodically thereafter until full remission is achieved; and (3) a plan should be developed that addresses the duration of antidepressant treatment.

[10] The Behavioral Health Autopsy Program (BHAP) Post-Mortem Chart Analysis Template (BHAP template) is a mechanism by which VA Central Office collects veteran suicide data from VAMCs' review of veterans' medical records. One BHAP template had been completed as of the time of our site visit, but had not been received by VA Central Office; therefore, we did not include this template in our review.

[11] Each VAMC is assigned to a single VISN.

[12] These symptoms include significant weight loss; insomnia or excessive sleeping; psychomotor agitation or retardation; fatigue or loss of energy; feelings of worthlessness or excessive or inappropriate guilt; diminished ability to think or concentrate, or indecisiveness; and recurrent thoughts of death, recurrent suicidal ideation without a specific plan, or a suicide attempt or a specific plan for committing suicide. American Psychiatric Association, *Diagnostic and Statistical Manual of Mental Disorders*, 5th ed. (Arlington, VA: American Psychiatric Association, 2013).

[13] Veterans Health Administration Handbook 1160.01, *Uniform Mental Health Services in VA Medical Centers and Clinics* (Sept. 11, 2008). The Handbook also requires that VAMCs provide evidence-based psychotherapy, such as Cognitive Behavioral Therapy, to veterans when appropriate. However, these services fall outside the scope of our review.

[14] The CPG also states that it is intended to "identify outcome measures to support the development of practice-based evidence that can ultimately be used to improve the clinical guidelines."

[15] The CPG is based on a review of research outcomes available at the time of publication. Evidence-based care refers to approaches that have consistently been shown in controlled research to be effective for a particular condition or conditions.

[16] The CPG for MDD is organized into 22 main topics, such as "initial treatment" and "treatment response." Each main topic contains a number of action statements that relate to approximately 200 recommendations for the management of veterans with MDD.

[17] The PHQ-9 is a diagnostic tool, which uses the nine MDD diagnosis symptoms as criteria to help clinicians make a criteria-based diagnosis of depressive disorders and measure depression severity to aid treatment decisions.

[18] The Veterans Crisis line can be reached by calling 1-800-273-8255 and pressing 1, online at www.VeteransCrisisLine.net, or sending a text message to 838255.

[19] Veteran suicide data is submitted by VAMCs to VA's Center of Excellence for Suicide Prevention located in VISN 2. The Center of Excellence was created by VA Central Office, and for the purposes of our report, we refer to the Center of Excellence as part of VA Central Office.

[20] As part of this initiative, VA collects veterans' demographic data, such as date of birth, date of death, race, ethnicity, and gender. VA also collects clinical data, such as the date of the veteran's final VA visit, whether the final visit was outpatient or inpatient, and the results of mental health screens, including depression screens.

[21] Prior to BHAPs, VA Central Office required suicide prevention coordinators to complete a review for suicide completions and attempts that identified, for example, the contributing factors for the event. Suicide prevention coordinators would then complete an aggregate analysis of all reported veteran suicides.

[22] VAMCs can also submit reviews for veterans who did not utilize VA health care services. Veterans not being seen within the VA will not have clinical information available in VA's medical records, but VAMCs can report information that is known through other mechanisms, such as a coroner's report or the veteran's family members, if available. According to VA, a comprehensive suicide prevention program requires timely and accurate information beyond that acquired from veterans being seen in VA. Data on these veterans are needed to, among other things, improve understanding of suicide among all veterans.

[23] Suicide prevention coordinators are responsible for asking family members if they are interested in participating in an interview. According to VA Central Office officials, a social worker at VA's Center of Excellence for Suicide Prevention conducts the family interview and multiple participants may be included in the interview.

[24] VAMC officials may send additional information to VISN and VA officials through issue briefs, which document specific factual information regarding unusual incidents, such as deaths, disasters, or anything else that happens at a VAMC, such as a veteran suicide, that might generate media interest or affect care. VAMCs are also required to complete peer reviews for suicides that occur within 30 days of any clinical encounter with a VA clinician. Peer review for quality management is used when there is a need to determine whether a provider's actions associated with an adverse event were clinically appropriate—that is, whether another provider with similar expertise would have taken similar action.

[25] This estimate is based on published Congressional Research Service data on the number of veterans who received health care services through VA from fiscal years 2009 through 2013 (roughly 5.5 million).

[26] These conflicts include Operation Iraqi Freedom, Operation Enduring Freedom, and Operation New Dawn.

[27] An encounter is a professional contact between a patient and a clinician in an outpatient or inpatient setting; a patient visit can consist of multiple encounters.

[28] Other depressive disorders include dysthymic disorder, adjustment disorder with depressed mood, and adjustment disorder with mixed anxiety and depressed mood.

[29] American Psychiatric Association: *Diagnostic and Statistical Manual.* Depression not otherwise specified is referred to in this edition as depressive disorder not otherwise specified.

[30] Officials at one VAMC in our review said that their facility conducts annual audits of nonbillable encounters, in part, to track the productivity of their providers and to maximize the amount of funding allocated to their facility by VA Central Office based on workload measures.

[31] For example, according to a VA Central Office official, if the clinician used the keyword search function and searched under the word "major depression", "major depressive disorder" would be returned as a possible diagnosis choice for selection. Currently, as a result of the software mapping error, if this selection is made, the encounter would be coded as depression not otherwise specified.

[32] *Uniform Mental Health Services in VA Medical Centers and Clinics* handbook.

[33] We reviewed five medical records from each of the six VAMCs we selected to determine whether veterans at these VAMCs were receiving care consistent with select recommendations from the CPG.

[34] Of these 5 veterans, 2 had treatment plans in the medical record that did not specify a time frame for follow up. One veteran returned in 7 weeks, as prescribed in the veteran's treatment plan. However, the remaining 2 veterans had a time frame in their treatment plan, but no explanation for why the follow-up encounter occurred outside this time frame. The first veteran's treatment plan instructed the veteran to return in 6 weeks; however, the veteran's follow-up encounter occurred approximately 12 weeks after the initial encounter. The second veteran's treatment plan instructed the veteran to return in 6-8 weeks, but the veteran was not seen until approximately 50 weeks after the initial encounter.

[35] As a result of our review, officials at one VAMC told us that they are developing plans to work with clinicians at the VAMC to implement measurement tools, including the PHQ-9.

[36] VA's Office of Inspector General (OIG) documented concerns about the timeliness of veterans' access to follow-up mental health care, which could affect the ability of veterans to receive follow-up with a clinician after beginning or changing antidepressant treatment. VA OIG, *Veterans Health Administration: Review of Veterans' Access to Mental Health Care* (Washington, D.C.: Apr. 23, 2012).

[37] In a June 2014 report, the Institute of Medicine also raised concerns with VA clinicians' adherence to CPG recommendations. This report reviewed the *VA/DOD Clinical Practice Guideline for Management of Post-Traumatic Stress* and stated that VA does not have a mechanism for the systematic collection and analysis of data for assessing the quality of care for post-traumatic stress disorder and that, as a result, VA often does not know whether veterans have received evidence-based treatments or whether these treatments are producing positive outcomes. The Institute of Medicine recommended that VA use evidence-based treatments as the treatment of choice for post-traumatic stress disorder, and these treatments should be delivered with fidelity to their established protocols. Institute of Medicine, *Treatment for Posttraumatic Stress Disorder in Military and Veteran Populations Report Brief* (Washington, D.C.: June 2014).

[38] VA's OMHO developed the psychopharmacology initiative in fiscal year 2014. This initiative is intended to address four areas: (1) possible overprescribing, (2) possible problems in clinical management, (3) misalignment between prescribing and diagnosis, and (4) missed opportunities. The metrics generally assess all veterans with any depression diagnoses, such as depression not otherwise specified; only one metric is specific to MDD. VA Central Office officials explained that data for this initiative are pulled from clinical and administrative records, but that extracting data can be challenging because, for example, clinicians may not be recording data in an extractable field in the medical record. VA Central Office officials also told us that they collect data on the number of veterans who receive 12-week and 6-month supplies of antidepressant medication, which relates to a CPG recommendation stating that, for veterans who achieve remission with antidepressants, treatment should be continued at the same dose for an additional 6- 12 months to decrease the risk of relapse. *VA/DOD Clinical Practice Guideline for Management of Major Depressive Disorder* (May, 2009) pg. 73.

[39] Specifically, these CPG recommendations state that veterans who are diagnosed with MDD should receive an initial trial of a single antidepressant, and that a second antidepressant medication may be considered for veterans who have had a partial response to treatment with one antidepressant. *VA/DOD Clinical Practice Guideline for Management of Major Depressive Disorder* (May, 2009). Other antidepressant metrics include: the proportion of veterans with depression receiving medication from three or more of four psychotropic classes (including antidepressants) for 60 or more continuous days; the proportion of inpatient or outpatient initial visits for new MDD diagnosis with antidepressant receipt

where there is no coverage for 84 days out of the first 114 days following the initial antidepressant fill; and the proportion of antidepressant prescriptions given with no medical or psychiatric indication. However, these metrics do not relate to specific recommendations in the CPG.

[40] VA also provides VAMCs data on the number of veterans screened annually using a standardized screening tool, a two item Patient Health Questionnaire (PHQ-2) and the percentage of veterans who screen positive for depression and have a timely suicide behavior evaluation completed. These measures meet CPG recommendations for annual screening for MDD and evaluation of suicide risk with a positive depression screen. Another mechanism VA uses to assess mental health care at VAMCs is site visits conducted by VA's OMHO. During these site visits, OMHO assesses, for example, how the number of veterans screened annually for depression compares to the national average as well as any trends within the VAMC. According to OMHO, the purpose of these site visits is to assess mental health care at individual VAMCs, specifically implementation and adherence to VA standards for mental health services. Once OMHO has identified both exemplary areas and areas for growth, OMHO then works with the mental health lead at the corresponding VISN to develop a strategic action plan for the VAMC, which will be monitored for implementation progress on a quarterly basis. However, these site visits do not look at specific CPG recommendations.

[41] Officials at one VAMC we visited told us that they use a clinical tool to track veterans being treated for mental health conditions. The mental health tool includes 67,349 unique patients, and an official explained that they can run queries of the clinical tool—for example, for veterans participating in substance abuse treatment who did not return for a drug screen—by pulling both process and outcome variables including diagnostic codes, lab results, and medication lists.

[42] VA policy states that VAMCs must have integrated mental health services that include co-located collaborative care and care management. Care management can be based on the BHL, Translating Initiatives for Depression into Effective Solutions (TIDES), or other evidence-based strategies approved by the Office of Mental Health Services. According to VA, TIDES facilitates collaboration between primary care clinicians and mental health specialists with support from a depression care manager, who, under the supervision of a mental health specialist, assists the primary care clinician in the assessment and ongoing management of depressed patients.

[43] According to officials at one VAMC we visited, clinicians previously used pharmacy data on a weekly basis to determine whether there were any veterans with new antidepressant orders from primary care who were not referred to the BHL. Officials told us that they stopped running the weekly query, since they consistently found that all eligible veterans had been referred to the BHL. However, in advance of our site visit, officials ran the query again and noted that some veterans were not being referred to the BHL. As a result, they plan to resume completing the weekly queries.

[44] We analyzed BHAP templates from five of the VAMCs at the time of our site visit or at the time we requested the BHAP templates. One VAMC had not completed any BHAP templates at the time of our site visit because they did not have a veteran die by suicide since the beginning of the BHAP initiative. Therefore, our analysis does not include BHAP templates from this VAMC.

[45] This field in the BHAP template states: "Is this case concerning a Veteran who was enrolled in VA Health Care Services?" For those veterans who were being seen in the VA, the box associated with this field should be checked.

[46] VA Central Office officials stated that this field could have become unchecked prior to submission of the template to Central Office, but that it was not the result of a programming error. For example, the box may have become unchecked after the VAMC official saved the template to a local location, but prior to the VAMC submitting the template to VA Central Office.

[47] According to one VA Central Office official, for the first interim report, officials matched veterans from the BHAP templates to medical record information to determine whether the veteran was receiving VA health care services.

[48] The 15 psychiatric symptoms in the BHAP template are isolation, anxiety, depressed mood, ruminations, suicidal ideation, sleep problems, intrusive memories, drug seeking behaviors, flashbacks, guilt/remorse, hallucinations, command suicide hallucination, alcohol withdrawal, agitation, and impulsivity.

[49] For example, the template answers for psychiatric symptoms originally included "yes" and "no." The template has been updated to also include "unknown," but this answer was not an option for all templates in our review. However, officials at two VAMCs provided us with the answers for fields that were left blank, including the fields for psychiatric symptoms.

[50] One VA Central Office official told us that for the first BHAP interim report, officials matched the number of suicide behavior reports to the number of BHAP templates using the veterans' social security numbers to determine that a BHAP template was submitted for each completed suicide behavior report. According to VA Central Office officials, this process was not conducted for the most recent BHAP interim report.

[51] We could not confirm date of death for two BHAP templates because the veterans' medical records did not contain a date of death. When confirming the lack of date of death in the medical records with the VAMC, officials stated that they took the date of death for one of the templates from the suicide behavior report. However, we did not find a suicide behavior report in the veteran's medical record.

[52] Two BHAP templates had dates of death that were 1 day off, one BHAP template was off by 3 days, and one BHAP template had a date of death off by 5 days.

[53] Although the BHAP template asks for the number of mental health visits, VA Central Office officials told us that they expect VAMCs to report mental health encounters, rather than visits. An encounter is a professional contact between a patient and a clinician in an outpatient or inpatient setting; a patient visit can consist of multiple encounters.

[54] According to VA Central Office officials, missing information in this field is treated as "0" in the interim report.

[55] The BHAP Guide can be used as a reference when completing the BHAP template because the BHAP Guide contains specific time frames for some of the fields, several of which are not outlined in the BHAP template.

[56] The BHAP Guide states that the final visit could include a mental health or a dental visit, but does not specify if a visit to an immunization clinic should be counted. The BHAP template includes a field for type of visit. One option as an answer for this field is "other," and the type of visit can be included in a text box in the template.

[57] VA Central Office has provided policy on the BHAP template through a memorandum and has also provided suicide prevention coordinators with a BHAP Guide, which explains how to fill out the BHAP template.

[58] In its comments on a draft of this report, VA stated that in September 2014 it provided guidance to VAMCs to complete BHAP templates for veterans not receiving VA services.

[59] See GAO, *Standards for Internal Control in the Federal Government*, GAO/AIMD-00-21.3.1 (Washington, D.C.: November 1999).

End Notes for Appendix I

[1] In general, veterans must enroll in VA health care to receive VA's medical benefits package, a set of services that includes hospital and outpatient services and prescription drugs. Veterans who served in the active military and who were discharged or released under conditions other than dishonorable may be eligible for VA health care. Some non-veterans may also be eligible for VA health care, such as spouses and children of veterans who have been rated permanently and totally disabled for a service-connected disability. We excluded non-veterans from our analysis.

[2] We identified this approach through discussions with VA clinical and data experts. This approach is consistent with previous GAO work. See, for example, GAO, *VA Mental Health: Number of Veterans Receiving Care, Barriers Faced, and Efforts to Increase Access*, GAO-12-12 (Washington, D.C.: Oct. 14, 2011).

[3] We were not able to further describe veterans by other eras of service, such as Vietnam, because according to a VA official, VA data on era of service are unreliable. DOD roster data was used to determine service in Operation Enduring Freedom, Operation Iraqi Freedom, and Operation New Dawn.

[4] Office of Management and Budget, *Provisional Guidance on the Implementation of the 1997 Standards for Federal Data on Race and Ethnicity* (Washington, D.C.: Dec. 15, 2000).

[5] Antidepressants, like other types of medications, may be used for off-label uses—that is, for a condition or patient population for which the drug has not been approved or in a manner that is inconsistent with information found on the approved drug label. For example, certain antidepressants may be used to treat anxiety and fibromyalgia. See K.J. Stone, A.J. Viera, and C.L. Parman, "Off-Label Applications for SSRIs" *American Family Physician,* vol. 68, no. 3 (2003).

[6] VA's approach to measuring its performance on these measures uses data regarding care rendered at VA facilities only; however, in order to account for care rendered by non-VA providers but paid for by VA, we incorporated fee basis data.

[7] The National Committee for Quality Assurance's 2013 antidepressant medication management quality measures are known as Effective Acute Phase Treatment and Effective Continuation Phase Treatment.

[8] Evidence-Based Practice Work Group. *VA/DOD Clinical Practice Guideline for Management of Major Depressive Disorder* (Washington, D.C.: May 2009).

[9] In contrast to the other site visits, which were completed in person, we completed the site visits to the VAMCs located in Gainesville, Florida, and Reno, Nevada, virtually through telephone interviews.

[10] VA assigns each VAMC a complexity score between 1 and 3, with level 1 being the most complex, using a facility complexity model. Level 1 is broken down further into 1a, 1b, and 1c. That model uses multiple variables to measure facility complexity arrayed along four categories, namely patient population served, clinical services offered, education and research complexity, and administrative complexity. Each VAMC is assigned to a single VISN.

[11] We use the phrase medical records to refer to electronic medical records.

[12] This approach for classifying veterans as having MDD is consistent with the approach used for the purposes of our data analysis, which we identified in discussions with VA.

[13] Veterans Health Administration Handbook 1160.01, *Uniform Mental Health Services in VA Medical Centers and Clinics* (Sept. 11, 2008).

[14] Although the guideline is not intended to define a standard of care, through policy, VA has set an expectation that providers follow the guideline's recommendations.

[15] For the purposes of this report, we refer to VAMCs to include community-based outpatient clinics.

[16] We also interviewed primary care and mental health providers at each community-based outpatient clinic.

[17] Veterans Health Administration Handbook 1160.01, *Uniform Mental Health Services in VA Medical Centers and Clinics* (Sept. 11, 2008).

[18] See GAO, *Standards for Internal Control in the Federal Government*, GAO/AIMD-00-21.3.1 (Washington, D.C.: November 1999) and GAO, *Internal Control Management and Evaluation Tool*, GAO-01-1008G (Washington, D.C.: August 2001).

[19] One template had been completed as of the time of our site visit, but had not been received by VA Central Office; therefore, we did not include this template in our review.

[20] Aspects of treatment paid for by VA, but rendered by non-VA providers (non-VA care) were not included in the scope of this review.

[21] We received additional templates from VA Central Office, but these were not analyzed because the VAMC had not provided us with templates for these veterans.

End Notes for Appendix II

[1] Veterans Health Administration Handbook 1160.01, *Uniform Mental Health Services in VA Medical Centers and Clinics* (Sept. 11, 2008).

[2] A safety plan is a prioritized written list of coping strategies and sources of support, such as individuals or agencies the veteran can contact, for the veteran to use during or preceding suicidal crisis in order to help lower the veteran's imminent risk of suicidal behavior. According to VA Central Office officials, the plan is created with clinician, veteran, and family interaction.

[3] Officials at this VAMC told us that their case managers are responsible for monitoring veterans flagged as being at high risk for suicide.

End Notes for Appendix III

[1] SPAN includes information on veterans, such as the number of suicide completions, the number of non-fatal suicide attempts, and other indicators of suicide prevention efforts. VAMC clinicians must complete a suicide behavior report when they learn that a veteran exhibited self-harming behavior and include that report in the respective veteran's medical record.

[2] Root cause analyses are used to identify the factors that contributed to adverse events or close calls and to identify any steps VAMCs could implement to prevent similar events in the future. Root cause analyses are completed under certain circumstances, such as when the act occurs during a VAMC inpatient stay or within 72 hours of being discharged from inpatient care.

[3] VISNs are regional networks of care. Each VAMC is assigned to a single VISN.

INDEX

A

B

C

M

N

O

P

Q

R

S